Alasdair Paine is a shi[...] [...]onized over Genesis 1–4 and yet has hidden that agony in such a deceptively clear and digestible style. He is preoccupied with 'What is God saying to us here?' and refuses to allow the elephant of secondary issues to stand between us and the Genesis text (though he provides additional notes for the curious). Here is a book I found refreshing my spirit, stimulating my mind, and nourishing my soul.

Dale Ralph Davis
Minister in Residence,
First Presbyterian Church, Columbia, South Carolina

Anyone seeking a wise, accessible guide to the crucial first chapters of Genesis need look no further. I found Alasdair's sure-footed work most illuminating and enriching.

Julian Hardyman
Senior Pastor, Eden Baptist Church, Cambridge

No section of the Bible is more fundamental than Genesis 1–4 and there is no better brief introduction to it than this. Alasdair Paine helpfully engages with the complex questions of interpretation but never gets bogged down in them. The focus throughout is God's contemporary message to us through these chapters, which is presented with great clarity and powerful application.

Vaughan Roberts
Rector of St Ebbe's Oxford and Director of Proclamation Trust

Don't let this book's brevity fool you. When I read I keep a pad at hand to record significant points. I recorded many pages' worth on reading *The First Chapters of Everything*. Alasdair Paine is an accomplished geographer, pastor and Bible student and all these disciplines add to the rich depth of his writing. Alasdair's insights, illustrations and sensitive application make this a very healthy read indeed. All of us need every encouragement to be regular, careful, prayerful readers of the Bible. This book gives such encouragement; it is the text which matters to this self-effacing author. So, pad at hand, here's a hearty read for the health of your soul.

David Cook
Retired Principal,
Sydney Missionary and Bible College, Sydney, Australia

ALASDAIR PAINE

THE FIRST CHAPTERS OF EVERYTHING

HOW GENESIS 1–4 EXPLAINS OUR WORLD

CHRISTIAN
FOCUS

Alasdair Paine is Vicar of St Andrew the Great, Cambridge and a trustee of Keswick Ministries.

Copyright © Alasdair Paine 2014

paperback ISBN 978-1-78191-323-9
epub ISBN 978-1-78191-358-1
mobi ISBN 978-1-78191-359-8

Published in 2014,
reprinted in 2015
by
Christian Focus Publications Ltd,
Geanies House, Fearn, Ross-shire,
IV20 1TW, Scotland, United Kingdom.
www.christianfocus.com

Cover design by Daniel van Straaten

Printed by
Bell and Bain, Glasgow

CONTENTS

Preface

I have written this book as a guide to the *message* of the Bible's momentous opening chapters. I hope it will be helpful to anyone wanting to get to grips with what Genesis 1–4 is about, whether regular Bible readers (you could perhaps use this with the passages as part of your daily readings), preachers, those investigating Christianity or anyone who finds these chapters a puzzle.

What this book is not
- A technical, academic commentary – there are some fine ones, of considerable length.

- An attempt to show the relationship between the opening chapters of Genesis and scientific discovery – again, there are many already (from different viewpoints).

- A guide to Christian ethics, taking these chapters as its starting point.

What it is

- An explanation of the message of the prologue (1:1–2:3) and first main section (2:4–4:26) of Genesis: what this tells us about God, ourselves and our world – and particularly how this relates to our lives today.

I started this work by preaching through Genesis 1–4 at Christ Church Westbourne, Dorset, and then again (afresh) at St Andrew the Great, Cambridge. Starting by preaching has three advantages.

- First and foremost, it approaches Genesis *as it should be approached*. I take it that this book was written as a message to be preached – as was the rest of the Bible! Persistently asking the question 'what is the message here?' is the correct way to handle the book. Much that is written on Genesis fails to do that – and so misses the point. Worse, it gets sidetracked into issues Genesis is not concerned with.

- Secondly, this approach proves remarkably fruitful in explaining *why Genesis is written as it is*. Many of the details puzzle us initially, but make complete sense when they are preached – for then we find that these chapters are deliberately shaped to convey particular points. We will see this again and again.

- Thirdly, this approach helps us see *how this book applies to us* – for proper preaching is always applied to our lives. Genesis was not given to satisfy our speculation but to bring us urgent truth about God, our world and ourselves.

Despite its enormous significance, it is hard to hear the message of Genesis 1–4 today. These chapters are widely dismissed as an ancient 'myth', a primitive account of origins long since displaced by scientific research. Within some churches, arguments about how to read the book (what are the 'days' of chapter 1, etc.?) have become so heated that we end up avoiding it. The result is the silencing of one of the most important messages of all time. This book is written out of a longing to make that message known.

For those seeking to work out the relationship between Genesis and science, I hope that this book, while not giving the answers, will at least give a steer as to what the Biblical text is about.

We have included the English Standard Version of the text of Genesis 1–4. I ask you to be like those noble Bereans in Acts 17:11, who checked what they heard against the Scriptures.

I dedicate this to Rachel, Tom, Lucy and Alice, and also to our church families, past and present – at Christ Church Westbourne, Bournemouth, and St Andrew the Great, Cambridge.

I am very grateful to various friends who have read drafts, commented and encouraged me to persevere: most notably Alec Motyer, Gordon Bridger, Julian Hardyman, Sean Jackson, Carl Laferton, Rachel Paine, Mike Symonds, Eleanor Trotter and my editors at Christian Focus, John van Eyk and Kate MacKenzie; and also to Billy McCurrie for allowing me to use his story in chapter 14.

I hope you will share my joyful sense of discovery.

Cambridge, Christmas 2013

1 The first chapters of everything

The opening chapters of Genesis interpret and account for universal human experience. They explain why life is such a strange mixture of the beautiful and the ugly, the happy and the tragic, the fulfilling and the frustrating. They show us why our world is orderly –the basic truth underpinning all science – and yet also strangely disordered. They dig into who we are, and what makes us distinctive as humans. They tell us what the good life is, and where to find it. Above all, they introduce us to God: not as a distant, hazy being but in breathtakingly sharp focus. Genesis shows how he made us to know him, but also how this most important of all relationships has gone wrong. And these chapters also hint of a solution which is more radical, intelligent and effective than we could ever have dreamt.

On the face of it, it would be a great surprise if anything so ancient (most likely over three thousand years old) could possibly speak usefully to us in the complexities of our lives. But we have it on the authority of Jesus Christ himself. His Hebrew Bible was the same as our Old Testament (the only difference being in the order of some books); it started with the book of Genesis, already very ancient in his own day. And it is clear that he regarded Genesis not just as the word of man, but as the Word of God. For instance, on an occasion when he was asked a tough ethical question, he answered by quoting two verses from Genesis as if they were *the* definitive word on the subject, and the ultimate author God himself.[1] In the same way, the New Testament as a whole looks back to Genesis again and again as authoritative, assuming it to be God's present word: my own edition of the Greek New Testament suggests no fewer than fifty-four points at which the New Testament touches on Genesis 1–4. If Genesis needs commendation – of the kind books often have on their covers – this is it!

The right approach

We start, however, with a problem: these early chapters of Genesis are surrounded by questions and controversies. Have they not, at least since the middle of the nineteenth century, been disproved by science? Isn't the Genesis account what people used to think – but which only flat-earthers believe now? To make matters worse, Christians themselves have differed in their response to this challenge, and there have been heated debates (in churches, schools, books and articles) about how science and Genesis are to relate. Some have said we can trust mainstream science; others, not. Sometimes these arguments have so overshadowed our reading of Genesis that they are all thinking of them when we read it. Inevitably – and sadly – there will be some who read this book whose main interest is not the explanation of the passages but which side this author is on!

In any piece of literature, surely the key to grasping it lies in understanding its *purpose*. What was Genesis written to convey? But rather than answering that question now, it is

---

1.. See Matthew 19:4-6, quoting Genesis 2:24 and attributing the narrative to the Creator himself.

better to be inductive: to start with the text of Genesis and work through it. At the end, I have a postscript, part of which addresses this question. But please take the guided tour first!

There are some difficult questions which are best dealt with as we go along, and I have included some extra sections at the end of some chapters to provide some tentative answers. I hope these are helpful, but they are much less important than the sections which take us through the text.

About Genesis

Genesis does not itself say who wrote it, but at the time of Jesus in the first century A.D., all the first five books of the Bible – the Pentateuch – were understood to be from Moses. Indeed, Jesus himself referred to the books of Exodus and Genesis in these terms,[2] and *Moses* is used in the New Testament as a shorthand for this section of the Bible.[3] This would locate its composition in the late Bronze Age, somewhere between the 1400s and 1200s B.C.

In the nineteenth and twentieth centuries A.D. this view was challenged, and the Pentateuch was widely held by scholars to be a later compilation of the work of various authors, some writing centuries after Moses. It might surprise a non-specialist, but these arguments were not based on dating ancient documents or tablets, but purely on aspects of literary style and vocabulary. For instance, it has been argued that Genesis 1:1–2:3 is a creation account by one author, and the account that begins in 2:4 is the work of another. The first calls God *Elohim*, and the second *Yahweh Elohim*. These, it is argued, reflect different eras and theological agendas. Based on the assumption that religion evolves through time, an attempt was then

---

2.. Mark 12:26; John 7:22

3.. Luke 24:27, 44

made to say which sections must have come earlier, and which later, in the history of Israel.

More recently, this view has itself been challenged, as it has been increasingly recognized that the criteria by which different bits of Genesis were assigned to different sources were in many cases subjective, with no hard external evidence; at the same time, a closer look at literary features of the account has demonstrated that it is indeed much more coherent than a multiple-source theory would suggest. We will see, as we go along, just how close that coherence is.

Moreover, it makes great sense that Genesis should have come from Moses' era. In later chapters of Genesis, customs are reported which make sense in the culture of the Bronze Age. The contents of Genesis are presupposed in other books of the Bible of great antiquity, such as Ezekiel and Micah.[4] And if the Bronze Age seems a long time ago – which it is – it is worth mentioning that there already existed accounts of creation given by the pagan nations surrounding ancient Israel, such as the Atrahasis Epic, dating to at least the seventeenth century B.C. Old Testament scholar John Collins concludes a thorough discussion of the issue: 'We also need not doubt that Moses was the primary author of the Pentateuch as we have it.'[5] That is not to say that Moses did not himself make use of even earlier source material.

Genesis was originally written in the Hebrew language. Contemporary translations such as the English Standard Version (the one in this book) are based on manuscripts dating from the medieval period, such as an important one in St Petersburg dating from the eleventh century A.D. Although this was a long time after the original documents, it has been

---

4. Ezekiel 33:24; Micah 7:20

5. C. J. Collins, *Genesis 1–4: A linguistic, literary and theological commentary* (Phillipsburg, NJ: P & R Publishing, 2006), p. 235.

shown by comparing manuscripts that the Hebrew scribes copied with meticulous care. To take one striking example, in 1947 a shepherd boy looking in a cave found the documents we now call the Dead Sea Scrolls. These included fragments of fifteen manuscripts of Genesis dating from the first century B.C. – over a thousand years before the medieval manuscripts. How similar would they be? 'These show few variants from the traditional text.'[6] We may have confidence that what we have in front of us really is Genesis!

Genesis was not originally written in chapters and verses, as now: those were added in the medieval period. Instead, it is divided into sections marked by the words *These are the generations of*, which come ten times in the book (for instance, in 2:4 and 5:1). The opening section (1:1–2:3) can be seen as a kind of prologue. This book covers this and the next section, up to the end of Genesis 4.

About this book

As the nineteenth-century Cambridge preacher Charles Simeon wrote, 'My endeavour is to bring out of Scripture what is there, and not to thrust in what I think might be there.'[7] What is sometimes rather grandly called 'interpretation' is really just a question of listening properly to the text, in its context. If you find yourself saying, 'that's just his interpretation,' please check Genesis for yourself – or the New Testament references which also help us understand it.

Following the convention of modern English translations, I have used the expression *the LORD* (capitalized) when reproducing the personal name of the God of the Bible, *Yahweh* in the Hebrew. Just remember that that is a name, not (as 'Lord' normally is in English) a title.

---

6.   G. J. Wenham, *Genesis 1–15* (Waco, Texas: Word Books, 1987), xxv.

7.   Quoted in Hugh Evan Hopkins, *Charles Simeon of Cambridge* (Sevenoaks: Hodder and Stoughton, 1977), p. 57.

GENESIS 1:1

In the beginning, God created the heavens and the earth.

2 In the beginning
Genesis 1:1

Christmas Eve, 1968. The spacecraft *Apollo 8* was orbiting the moon for the very first time. No humans had ever ventured so far from our planet; no mortal eyes had ever before seen the earth rising in the distance, a beautiful cloud-swathed ball of blue above the grey lunar horizon.

As the world watched and listened, the crew broadcast a live Christmas message. After commenting on the awe-inspiring view from the capsule window, they read out the first ten verses of Genesis, in the King James translation. 'In the beginning', we heard William Anders say against the hiss and crackle, 'God created the heaven and the earth. And the earth was without form, and void ... and God said, let there be light...' The words had an astonishing, unforgettable resonance. Here was humanity experiencing the grandeur of the universe in a completely new way, and we were hearing from the book which introduces its Maker. Later, the crew won an Emmy for their broadcasts.

So we come to the simple, momentous words with which Genesis starts, each packed with implications. In this chapter we will get no further than the very first verse; but was there ever a single sentence that said so much?

'In the beginning...'

The little phrase *In the beginning* may not catch our attention in its own right, but it should. The very claim that there was a *beginning* sets Genesis apart from those worldviews which see the universe as everlasting. In the 1950s, for instance, many cosmologists held to the 'Steady State' theory of the universe: that it has always existed (a theory now largely replaced by the idea of a hot Big Bang, which, of course, is all about a beginning). In similar vein, some Eastern religions understand time as essentially cyclical and ultimately directionless. But in strong contrast, Genesis asserts that there was a beginning to the universe we inhabit.

If we say that the universe had an absolute beginning, that means that its history is best seen as a line, rather than a circle. And that raises the question: 'Where is the line pointing?' The answer to that will come later, but already we have a hint that our universe has a purpose, and life has a direction and meaning. The Bible will go on to say much more about this.

'...God created the heavens and the earth'

Even more importantly, Genesis asserts that there is a God, who brought the universe into existence. The expression *The heavens and the earth* is deliberately all-inclusive: there is not a postal address anywhere in the cosmos which does not have one or the other as its bottom line. God made all that! The galaxies, the black holes, the earth, the rainforests, incy-wincy spider, you, me, everyone. He is not the result of our imagination; we are the result of his.

And what imagination! I am writing this in August, and last night we popped out to look for the annual Perseids meteor shower. Not being astronomers, we were just watching for the fun of it. We live in a built-up area, so weren't able to see this in all its glory, but still caught some glimpses of the shooting stars as they streaked across the sky. Near the southern horizon, Jupiter glowed brightly, three of its moons twinkling in my binoculars. Our son was telling us, meanwhile, about the fireflies he had seen at summer camp. It was a moment of wonder. We all know times like that. Truly we live in a world 'charged with the grandeur of God'.[1] We rightly look at it and think, who must he be, and what must he be like, to have made all this? As the Psalmist says, 'The heavens declare the glory of God'.[2] The sound of the surf pounding the beach, the smell of heather, the taste of honey, the music of the skylark, the intricacy of a spider's web, the soaring heights of the mountains covered with snow – who must he be, to have thought of all that?

The Hebrew word for *created* (*bara*) is a loaded one. Hebrew scholar Alec Motyer explains that within the Old Testament, 'When the verb "to create" has a subject, it is always God; when it has a presumed subject, it is always God... it is used throughout the Old Testament of acts or events which either by their speciality or novelty or both point to God as their originator.'[3] It is a word which comes specially here in verse 1, and recurs in the chapter only at specially emphatic points: in verse 21 (the creation of life) and verse 27 (humanity); in most of the chapter, the verb is the more normal 'made'. In creating, God is doing something here that only he can do. For creation involves more than simply refashioning something: it is about establishing the very principles by which something exists.

---

1. Gerard Manley Hopkins, 'God's Grandeur' (1877).

2. Psalm 19:1

3. Alec Motyer, *Look to the Rock* (Leicester: IVP, 1996), p. 67.

It is sometimes said that the statement 'God created' begs the question 'who created God?'. But this God was already there *in the beginning*: he is eternal and uncreated. So the question needs no answer. If that sounds like a cop-out, remember that those who deny God's existence also believe in what is eternal and uncreated: they just call it matter, energy or natural laws. We have, in a sense, to choose who or what we think was always there; and is there any good reason why we should think it was just matter?

Coming back to the text, verse 1 may refer to an initial act of creation, followed by the sequence described from verse 2 onwards; or it may simply be a headline for the whole first chapter of Genesis. Either is possible. But whichever is correct, what we cannot escape is that verse 1 affirms that God has created the heavens and the earth. This is how it is understood in that ancient statement of faith of the Christian church, the Apostles' Creed, which alludes to these very words when it says, 'I believe in God the Father Almighty, Creator of Heaven and Earth.'

'Prove it!'

At this point, we might want Genesis to answer an obvious question. We have just heard a statement which is often challenged – that there is a God, who made everything. So will Genesis prove it? There are, of course, many clues which point this way, such as those well surveyed by Timothy Keller in his book *The Reason for God*:

> the very fact that the universe had a beginning; the astonishing fine-tuning of the universe's physical constants, allowing life to develop; the regularity and beauty of nature; the very fact that we have rationality at all.[4]

---

4.   Timothy Keller, *The Reason for God* (New York: Dutton, 2008), ch. 8; see also John Lennox, *God's Undertaker: Has Science Buried God?* (Oxford: Lion, 2007).

These are all pointers to a Creator.

Genesis, however, just doesn't seem interested in evidence of this kind. You may find that frustrating. But I take it that this is not because such reasoning is unimportant, but because Genesis has a different agenda. The focus of the creation account is not on God's fingerprints, but on God himself.

Some years ago, we had the unexpected excitement of hosting a police stake-out at our house. The detectives, who spent a great deal of time in our bedroom peering through the curtains at some people over the road, had all kinds of gadgetry for their surveillance. I found the process fascinating: the video cameras, the way they were able to snoop without being seen, and so on. But, of course, *their* interest lay not in their technology or methods, but in the suspects they were watching. Similarly, Genesis is wanting to move us beyond the evidence for a Maker to meet him for ourselves. That, of course, can only happen if he introduces himself – which is what is happening here.

This is important at a personal level. It is surprising how many people are satisfied when their thoughts about God stop with a vague notion of a Great Architect or Ultimate Being, without wanting to know more. They may be interested in the evidence for God, but leave things there. But if there is a God who made the universe, can it be right to rest with such fuzzy notions? How woefully unsatisfying and inadequate! How little nourishment that would ever bring our souls! Instead, shouldn't we want to know all about this most awesome person? That is why Genesis takes us to meet our Maker, as we will see as we go on to explore the rest of chapter 1.

The Bible is always doing that.

Some practical implications

Before getting there, it is worth pausing on Genesis' first verse, because later parts of the Bible keep dwelling on the great truths it contains, applying them to us in various practical ways. In no sense is this teaching about God creating the heavens and the earth a merely theoretical truth: it should make a difference to our lives today.

For one thing, this verse should make us **value the wisdom of God**. The book of Proverbs extols God's wisdom, and exhorts us to seek it. It appeals to creation, as wisdom herself speaks:

> The LORD possessed me at the beginning of his work,
>> the first of his acts of old...
> When there were no depths I was brought forth,
>> when there were no springs abounding with water...
> When he established the heavens, I was there...[5]

The point is simple: it was by means of his wisdom that God created the universe; and what wisdom that was! So:

> And now, O sons, listen to me:
>> blessed are those who keep my ways.
> Hear instruction and be wise, and do not neglect it.[6]

We will profit if we listen to God's wisdom, because it is truly very wise! Proverbs is assuming, of course, that the God who speaks in the rest of the Bible is the same as the Creator (which is something Genesis will go on to assert). If so, we have access to the same wisdom by which our world was made. Even if it sounds like an oversimplification, it is profoundly right to call the Bible

---

5.   Proverbs 8:22, 24, 27

6.   Proverbs 8:32-33

'The Maker's Instructions'; what a gift to have wisdom from the One who made everything!

As Genesis introduces God to us, the **terms of our relationship** are also being established. They can hardly be said to be equal. This God just happens to have created the heavens and the earth. Just who are we, in comparison? This is a lesson which, in our pride, we constantly need to relearn, just as the prophet Isaiah's contemporaries had to:

> Thus says the LORD,
> > the Holy One of Israel, and the one who formed him
> > [humanity]:
> Ask me of things to come;
> > will you command me concerning my children and
> > the work of my hands?
> I made the earth and created man on it;
> it was my hands that stretched out the heavens, and
> > I commanded all their host.[7]

It seems that the people Isaiah was addressing were arguing with God, and even thinking they knew better. Understanding that he is the creator should put them back in their place.

At the church we belonged to when we lived near London, there used to be a moment in Sunday services set aside for saying hello to the person sitting next to you. In a big church, this was a way to help everyone get to know each other and break a bit of British reserve. There was a conversation between a young man and a more senior one sitting next to him. 'What do you do?', the young man asked. 'I'm in the legal profession,' the other replied. 'So am I!', replied the younger man, and went on to give his views about the state of the law. Afterwards,

---

7.   Isaiah 45:11-12

a friend went up and said to the younger man, 'I hope you enjoyed talking to the Lord Chancellor.' Time for a red face! The younger man had been telling the head of the English legal system how to do his job.

We do that with God, don't we? Genesis will go on to show us the wretched consequences of that attitude. But it should have been ruled out of court by the very first verse of the book. As we meet this God, we can only do so with due humility, with reverence, with awe. The first verse of Genesis shows us God in his proper place; by implication, it also begins to show us ours.

This is also the God **to whom his people pray**. In desperate days, with his home city under siege, the prophet Jeremiah prayed: 'Ah, LORD God! It is you who has made the heavens and the earth by your great power and by your outstretched arm! Nothing is too hard for you.'[8] Against his bleak situation, Jeremiah set the creator God. If he has made the universe, can anything be too hard for him? Perhaps the greatest secret of prayer is knowing the one we pray to, and the astonishing privilege of the Christian is being in covenant, as Jeremiah was, with the one who created everything. Ponder that, and remember the might and power of the one we are speaking to. Can any problem we face be too big for the God who *created the heavens and the earth*?

This great truth also **spells no to 'God in a box'**. In Acts 17, we read of the Apostle Paul's preaching in Athens in the first century A.D. His audience was both learned and religious, but there was something they had got badly wrong:

---

8.   Jeremiah 32:17

> The God who made the world and everything in it, being Lord of heaven and earth, does not live in temples made by man, nor is he served by human hands, as though he needed anything, since he himself gives to all mankind life and breath and everything.[9]

Athenian religion, it seems, had made the classic mistake of confining God to shrines and places of worship, and thinking that he somehow needs our help. On the contrary, the true and living God is maker of all, asserts Paul: so it is not he who needs our help, but we his! Indeed, our very next breath comes from him. He is Lord of heaven and earth, so he can hardly be confined, either. He is the God of all of life.

Any survey of world religion will show that it seems to be a very common human tendency to confine God: to sacred places or to needing our help. We have to go to a special building to pray, we think; or we feel he wants us to do a favour by putting a bit in the collection or donating our old piano to the church. But if he is the creator of heaven and earth, the tables are turned!

Finally, this is the God **to whom the entire universe belongs**, for he made all of it: *the heavens and the earth*. That gives him ownership rights over everything and everyone – including you. Paul needed to say this in Athens, for a culture which had forgotten that God is the creator of all slipped easily into thinking 'Your way is fine for you, and my way is fine for me.' Genesis also needed to say it, because it, too, was written in a world of many faiths. Genesis 1:1 has us know that there is one, true, living Creator God, who has ownership rights over

---

9. Acts 17:24-25

everything and everyone. Whoever you are, whatever your present views of all this, whether you call yourself a Christian or not: if you happen to live in either the heavens or the earth, what you are about to read has to do with you.

²The earth was without form and void, and darkness was over the face of the deep. And the Spirit of God was hovering over the face of the waters.

³And God said, 'Let there be light', and there was light. ⁴And God saw that the light was good. And God separated the light from the darkness. ⁵God called the light Day, and the darkness he called Night. And there was evening and there was morning, the first day.

⁶And God said, 'Let there be an expanse in the midst of the waters, and let it separate the waters from the waters.' ⁷And God made the expanse and separated the waters that were under the expanse from the waters that were above the expanse. And it was so. ⁸And God called the expanse Heaven. And there was evening and there was morning, the second day.

⁹And God said, 'Let the waters under the heavens be gathered together into one place, and let the dry land appear.' And it was so. ¹⁰God called the dry land Earth, and the waters that were gathered together he called Seas. And God saw that it was good.

¹¹And God said, 'Let the earth sprout vegetation, plants yielding seed, and fruit trees bearing fruit in which is their seed, each according to its kind, on the earth.' And it was so. ¹²The earth brought forth vegetation, plants yielding seed according to their own kinds, and trees bearing fruit in which is their seed, each according to its kind. And God saw that it was good. ¹³And there was evening and there was morning, the third day.

¹⁴And God said, 'Let there be lights in the expanse of the heavens to separate the day from the night. And let them be for signs and for seasons, and for days and years, ¹⁵and let them be lights in the expanse of the heavens to give light upon the earth.' And it was so.

[16]And God made the two great lights—the greater light to rule the day and the lesser light to rule the night—and the stars. [17]And God set them in the expanse of the heavens to give light on the earth, [18]to rule over the day and over the night, and to separate the light from the darkness. And God saw that it was good. [19]And there was evening and there was morning, the fourth day.

[20]And God said, 'Let the waters swarm with swarms of living creatures, and let birds fly above the earth across the expanse of the heavens.' [21]So God created the great sea creatures and every living creature that moves, with which the waters swarm, according to their kinds, and every winged bird according to its kind. And God saw that it was good. [22]And God blessed them, saying, 'Be fruitful and multiply and fill the waters in the seas, and let birds multiply on the earth.' [23]And there was evening and there was morning, the fifth day.

[24]And God said, 'Let the earth bring forth living creatures according to their kinds—livestock and creeping things and beasts of the earth according to their kinds.' And it was so. [25]And God made the beasts of the earth according to their kinds and the livestock according to their kinds, and everything that creeps on the ground according to its kind. And God saw that it was good.

3 Meet your Maker

Genesis 1:2-25

I would love to hear a great actor like Kenneth Branagh or Meryl Streep read the opening chapter of Genesis. The sheer beauty of its language echoes the beauty of the creation it describes. There is a majestic, orderly calm in the refrain *And there was evening, and there was morning*, reflecting the orderly calm of the Creator going about his work. The economy of style is amazing, yet the mind's eye is full of pictures: of light, of dark, of seas, of continents, of stars, of plants and trees and great sea creatures, of birds and livestock and wild animals. It is not poetry in the strict sense, but the writer has taken a poet's care with words.

In fact, the more one studies the whole opening section, which runs up to Genesis 2:3, the more one realises how carefully – indeed ingeniously – it has been written. For instance, commentators have noticed that the whole passage is dominated by multiples of seven. The first sentence (1:1) is seven words long in the Hebrew; the expression *And God made* comes seven times; God's name is mentioned thirty-five times – and more.[1] This is clearly deliberate, and ought to intrigue us. There is also a pattern to what happens on the different days, with the events of the first three being mirrored in the events of the second three. Then there is the numbering, with the sequence of days creating a sense of anticipation. And so on.

All this points to the fact that this account, despite its great antiquity, is no primitive ragbag. Each word has been weighed, each sentence carefully crafted. Clues have been laid to the meaning throughout, which we are expected to spot. The writer's care emphasizes the importance of the topic.

Twenty-first-century readers of the passage find themselves perplexed – and distracted – by the question of what the 'days' of creation mean. Are they earth days, or something else? Do they contradict what science says about the age of the universe? Why are they such a prominent feature of the account anyway? Their significance (and the importance of the number seven) will become clearer when we reach the seventh day, so I ask for your patience until we get there. Genesis' first priority is to introduce to us the hero of the account.

God: the hero of the account

One great figure dominates this whole account: the Creator himself. He is the subject of more than two-thirds of the sentences. This is both deliberate and important. Genesis was written in a world of many faiths: in the religious supermarket of the Ancient Near East there were religions with animal gods, gods of the

---

1. G. J. Wenham, *Genesis 1–15* (Waco: Word, 1987), p. 6.

heavenly bodies, fertility gods, gods of war, and more. In our own multi-faith world, with the major religions jostling alongside each other, the confusion is arguably even greater. It is all very well to say that we believe in God, but what exactly do we mean by that term? 'I like to think of God as...' is a common answer, but are we right? Although at one level Genesis 1 is about our world, it is first and foremost giving us a vital primer about the one who made it. It is only a first introduction, but first introductions tend to be rather important.

He is personal: he speaks (calling things into being), he sees (that what he has made is good), he acts (making things), he gives names (calling what he has made sea, sky, earth), he blesses (the animals and people), he takes pleasure (seeing that it is all very good). In Genesis 2, he rests. These are things that persons do; he is not just a force. That is why Christians speak of a 'Personal God'.

This is a contrast to the way God has sometimes been understood. The deists of the eighteenth century spoke of God as a force or first cause – but really no more.[2] Radical theologians of the 1960s used the term 'the ground of our being'.[3] Some religions are happy to talk about God or the gods, but can only express the relationship mechanically, for instance by means of prayer flags or wheels. Or we find ourselves talking about fate: a blind, impersonal thing controlling our lives, or a 'something' that is there. The truth is that none of these beings are really personal. Maybe in sophisticated Western society

---

2. See James W. Sire, *The Universe Next Door* (Downers Grove, IL: IVP, 4th edition, 2004) ch. 3.

3. See John A. T. Robinson and David L. Edwards, *The Honest to God Debate* (London: SCM, 1963).

we prefer such impersonal entities because they sound more 'scientific', or because we find a 'force' rather less threatening than a real person. In Genesis, however, the ultimate Controller of the universe is one who is watching me as I write, and you as you read. That is why Genesis is so keen to introduce us to God. He is not just a thing but a person who can be known.

One morning I overheard my wife talking very slowly and deliberately on the phone. There were long pauses and a strange absence of small talk. Who on earth was Rachel speaking to? It was a computer. She was buying some cinema tickets on the automated booking line. I suppose it's convenient, but don't we far prefer talking to a real person? The great news is that the universe is not run by impersonal forces, nor can the living God ever possibly be described that way. He is a person.

Nowhere is God's personhood clearer than that he **speaks**. *And God said* comes again and again (1:3, 6, 9, 11, 14, 20, 24, 26, 29). Again and again, the Bible wants us to know that: the expression *The word of the Lord* comes no fewer than 258 times in Scripture. This is a truth about God foundational enough to be stressed at the very first introduction, here in Genesis 1. And it is a truth that should make us prick up our ears. For if God is personal, and speaks, this opens up the possibility of relationship with him. He is not silent; he may be known, because he speaks.

And look what happens when he does: a universe springs into being. We are being introduced to the one whose words are powerful beyond our imaginings.

Genesis also introduces God as being in **absolute, sovereign control**. This is emphasized by the repeated formula *And God saw that* [what he had created] *was good.*

Not only does that tell us that creation is good; it also tells us that it came out just as God wanted it to come out. Precisely.

From time to time I have to do some DIY round our home. Sadly, not every shelf I put up is entirely straight. The truth is that when I stand back and look at my work, I cannot always say 'It is good'. Sometimes it verges on being quite good, I admit. But *very* good (Gen. 1:31)? That is what God says of his work: it came out exactly as he wanted it to.[4]

God's control is also emphasized by the fact that he only has to speak for things to happen. *And God said... and it was so.* That is power. Picture the situation at your workplace when there is a visit from the management. The boss and all the big hitters are there. One of them sniffs a bad drain. They only need to say the word, and a little army of people are out there with shovels and rods. The management's clout is reflected in the fact that only a word is needed.[5]

And look what God controls. He gathers together whole oceans (9); his making the stars is described almost as an afterthought (16). In verse 21, we are told that he made 'the great sea creatures, and every living thing with which the waters swarm'. Gordon Wenham translates *sea creatures* as *monsters*, and points out that the verb *swarm* refers normally only to little things.[6] The point is that even the biggest, scariest things in the sea are small fry to the sovereign God; the great white shark in *Jaws* is like a minnow to him.

---

4. For a further example of the way Genesis emphasizes this, compare v. 11 (what God said) with v. 12 (what happened).

5. Phillip D. Jensen, *The Genesis Tapes* (Sydney, St Matthias, 1990).

6. Wenham, *Genesis 1–15*, p. 24.

Who, or what, controls our world and our lives? It may be that the reference to *the stars* in verse 16 is an implied criticism of astrology, the ancient belief that the heavenly bodies somehow control our destinies. Millions continue to look to this for guidance in their daily lives. But if God made the stars, that puts the signs of the zodiac in their proper places. Why not look beyond them to the Creator of the heavens and the earth? Converts to Christianity find themselves putting horoscopes behind them and discovering, in the pages of the Bible, the one who really is in control. Isn't he the one to trust?

Note also that in Genesis 1 there is **only one God**. There is no scope for polytheism, the view that there are lots of deities. Genesis is strikingly different at this point from other creation accounts of the ancient Middle East. For instance, in the eightennth-Century-B.C. *Epic of Atrahasis*, an old Babylonian account of creation, heaven is ruled by the god Anu, the earth by Enlil and the waters under the earth are ruled by Enki; other, minor, gods work in the fields.[7] In Genesis there is no mention of other gods, and none of the partitioning of the heavens and earth (with one god ruling this bit, and another that) that is inevitable if you do have different gods. With majestic simplicity, Genesis tells us of just one almighty Creator, who is Lord of everywhere and everything. He is supreme and unrivalled. And there is not even a hint of dualism, the view that there are equal and opposite forces of good and evil, as if history were a boxing match between both sides, with an uncertain outcome.

---

7.   www.britishmuseum.org/explore; search under 'Atrahasis Epic'.

Mention of the Spirit of God (2) and the plural form *let us* in verse 26 do hint, intriguingly, at a plurality. It is only a hint, and the rest of the Bible will have much more to say about this, as we are introduced to God as Trinity. But this plurality is *within* God and not external to him.

As the only God, God is in total control. That is a truth that should make those who seek to avoid him tremble. But it should also help God's friends sleep at night.

The God who shines his light

There is one more striking truth about God, which comes right at the beginning of the section. At first sight, verse 2 is a puzzle: 'The earth was without form and void, and darkness was over the face of the deep.' The picture is of desolation, emptiness, or, as Gordon Wenham translates it, 'total chaos';[8] combined with *darkness* and *the deep,* there is a disorderly, even frightening, feel. Jeremiah uses the same word-picture to describe a scene of total devastation.[9] What does this refer to? Some kind of primeval soup of half-made creation? Genesis tells us tantalizingly little. But what is clear is that this description is intended as a prelude to what happened next. 'And the Spirit of God was hovering over the face of the waters. And God said, "Let there be light", and there was light.' Out of this chaos, the Creator God brings order.

This is significant. For one thing, the picture of primeval chaos reminds us not to take the orderliness

---

8.   Wenham, *Genesis 1–15*, p. 15; though we must be careful, because 'chaos' is a Greek, not a Hebrew, word and concept.

9.   Jeremiah 4:23

of our world for granted. We will see in the next chapter that this ordered nature of creation is a big theme here. It could have been otherwise; indeed, in the narrative of the flood (Gen. 6–9), God's judgment is to return things, temporarily, to watery chaos. We should read verse 2 with a sense of relief that God, in his goodness, has not left it like this.

But there is a deeper message here. For don't we live in a world where the disorder and chaos caused by human behaviour are our common experience? I suppose it would be possible to conceive of a God who creates but then leaves things. He would be of little practical use to us in the hash we find ourselves in. But the Creator of the universe is also revealed here in the opening sentences of Genesis to be the one who brings illumination and order to a dark and desolate world.

Could it be that he also does this to dark and desolate lives? The Apostle Paul thought so. He wrote to the church in Corinth, 'For God, who said, "Let light shine out of darkness", has shone in our hearts to give the light of the knowledge of the glory of God in the face of Jesus Christ.'[10] As Paul talks about God's great power to change lives, he goes right back to this opening picture from creation itself.

One of the perks of my job, as a Christian minister, is to see this, in real lives today. It is truly wonderful hearing and seeing the way the Son of God changes a person's life as they turn to him in trust. Next time you hear someone speak of the difference Jesus Christ has made to them, think of Genesis 1:2. The dark fog of unbelief is

---

10. 2 Corinthians 4:6

replaced by a new clarity of vision; alienation from God is replaced by a living friendship; lives disordered by sin are reordered by God's Spirit. This verse is the first hint of the Christian good news in the Bible.

Are we a bit too early in Genesis to be talking of God's capacity to reorder broken lives? After all, we don't get on to a world that needs rescuing until Genesis 3. But perhaps Genesis just cannot wait to start pointing us to the God who alone can deal with the state we are in. For a messy world *is* where we live, and any thoughtful person will long for an answer. It is as if Genesis is hinting that being a sorter-out is so fundamental to God's very nature that it is almost the first thing we need to hear about him.

Some years ago, the church I serve in Cambridge had a major building project. A huge banner hung on the outside, telling all the passers-by that WE RESTORE BUILDINGS, BUT GOD RESTORES LIVES. This was not hype, but the truth. For the God we are talking about is the one who says, *Let there be light.*

4 The world about us

More from Genesis 1:2-25

Sitting on the coach to the airport is a man taking time out for a trip to South America to campaign against deforestation. He thinks of the world, and particularly the forest, as intrinsically divine. The destruction of the rainforest is a violation of that sacredness. His trip is a spiritual campaign: he regards himself as a deeply spiritual person.

A few rows back is the head of a small biotechnology company. She has no interest in that kind of superstition. She revels in the fact that the world is ordered and explicable, for the profitability of her business has stemmed from the success of its science. She is an atheist, and the main reason she gives for this is the progress of science: as knowledge of the world has advanced, religion has retreated: 'Acts of God' have been explained in purely natural terms.

Also on the coach sits a man heading for an ashram in the East. In his spiritual pilgrimage, he has come to think of the physical world as essentially evil; he wants to find himself, and God, by escaping this world's trappings. He wants to meet holy men who live on almost nothing, that he might learn from them. His is the smallest suitcase on the coach!

At the back – and creating most of the noise – is a party of girls heading for a hen weekend on a sun-soaked beach. Right now, they aren't particularly interested in any of the above. At least as far as this weekend is concerned, it doesn't much matter whether there's a God in charge of the world, or even what sort of world it really is. It's time for some fun.

My apologies for the stereotypes. But we do think of the world in a variety of very different ways, don't we? Different world views lead to different lifestyles, and even different cultures. Underlying many debates about ethics or politics are differences of understanding about the fundamental nature of reality.

Genesis 1 has much to say about all this – inevitably so, since it is about creation. It radically challenges some contemporary world views, just as it did the world views of its time. We have seen its headlines about God; what are its headlines about the world, the universe, and us?

Four truths about the universe

Perhaps most obviously, Genesis 1 asserts that **creation depends on God**. Everything – heavens, earth, day, night, sea, sky, sun, stars, plants and animals – is explicitly said to be his handiwork. None of it would be here without him. The universe is not a self-contained system that has spawned itself.

When my parents celebrated a big wedding anniversary, I was glad to be able to say to them, 'Thank you for having me: I wouldn't be here without you.' The creation must say the same of its Creator; and if this seems obvious to us, it is only because we have inherited a Judaeo-Christian world view, derived from Genesis. For many in the world, these truths are not obvious at all.

This is the foundation of the Bible doctrine of providence, which says that the world *continues* to depend on him. As the Apostle Paul put it when he was explaining Christianity in first-century Athens: God 'himself gives all men life and breath and everything else.'[1] Your very next breath depends on him; so do the atoms in your body, the gravity that sticks you to the earth, the food that you eat. Genesis 1 should prompt a proper humility and thankfulness in all areas of life.

Equally, the universe is **distinct from God**. *In the beginning, God...* (1:1), is how Genesis starts. God is there first; creation comes next. Creation owes its existence to him, but is not him. It comes into being at God's command, but God is not one with it, as if he were part of it (or even the sum total of it). Genesis' worldview is thus quite different from the whole set of worldviews (ancient as well as contemporary) which belong in the file marked 'pantheism': the idea that there is a bit of God in you, me, the trees, the hills or elsewhere in the world. Certainly we should value creation. But its value stems from the fact that it is the work of its Creator, not that it has the place of the Creator. We enjoy the creation, but are not to worship it. How tragically misguided that would be: how could relating to a sacred tree or stone ever compare with knowing the living God?

---

1. Acts 17:25, NIV

In a sense this is an easy mistake to make. The glories of the universe are so great that it is easy to make them objects of worship. A gorgeous sunset, soaring mountains, the rumble of thunder or ancient trees can be breathtaking and inspiring, and so we can easily persuade ourselves that they should be a substitute for God in our affections. But this is not a noble exchange. It means stopping short of God himself, of all he is and may require of us. The Bible has a word for it: idolatry.[2] The creation is marvellous, but is not God. Its glory points to his glory, so that we might come to know him. Never settle for less.

Genesis also insists that **the creation is good**. Seven times between 1:1 and 2:3 we are told this. The word for *good* can also be translated *beautiful*.[3] The summary at the end of the passage makes sure we've got the point: 'And God saw everything that he had made, and behold, it was very good.'

Again, this may seem obvious, but for millions it is not. Some religions teach that the physical world is intrinsically evil, so really holy people do their best to escape it. They may shun clothing or food, because asceticism is the route to enlightenment. It is regarded as more godly to be single than married, and poverty is even held to be a virtue!

Not if Genesis has anything to do with it. For God invented the physical world, and he says it is good. Next time you throw a ball on the beach, taste fresh vegetables or enjoy a sunset, thank him for it. He thought of it, and

---

2. See Romans 1:18–32 for some consequences of this attitude.

3. V. P. Hamilton, *Genesis 1–17* (Grand Rapids: Eerdmans, 1990) p. 120.

he gave it to us. He even gave us the taste buds to enjoy the food. How sad it is, then, when stinge-mongers pop up and tell us that the godly way to live is to reject all this. It seems they have been around – within the churches as well as in other religions – for a long time. The Apostle Paul was talking about these sorts of people when he wrote his first letter to Timothy. They 'forbid marriage and require abstinence from foods that God created to be received with thanksgiving', writes Paul; and as he shows how wrong they are, it is to Genesis 1 that Paul goes: 'For everything created by God is good, and nothing is to be rejected if it is received with thanksgiving...'[4] The fact is that many people assume that Christians are against our enjoyment of the world. If there is any substance in that accusation, those Christians should have paid attention to Genesis.

The goodness of the physical world which God has created also underpins the desire of Christians to care physically for others. It is there behind Christian concerns for body as well as soul; it underpins the foundation of every mission hospital or the many times Jesus told his followers to give to the poor.[5]

One of the biggest themes of Genesis 1 is that **the creation is orderly**. This is true both of the activity of creation and the finished product. God's whole work of creating is, in a sense, one of creating order. From the earth being *without form and void* (2), God separates light from darkness (4), the seas from the clouds (7) and the oceans from the continents (9). When the land produces

---

4.   1 Timothy 4:1-4
5.   For example, Mark 10:21, Luke 12:33

vegetation, it reproduces with the predictability that comes from orderliness:

> The earth brought forth vegetation, plants yielding seed according to their own kinds, and trees bearing fruit in which is their seed, each according to its kind (12).

The sun and moon are created for the regularity which comes with orderliness, acting as giant clocks (17-18). The very pattern of the days (with the pattern of the first three days mirrored in the fourth to sixth days) stresses orderliness.[6] In all sorts of ways, Genesis 1 is driving home to us the orderliness of creation. It is, quite literally, sorted.

When I was a small boy, a favourite book was the *I-Spy Book of Astronomy*. It contained quiz questions to make sure its little readers had got the facts. One of them was 'When will be the next total eclipse of the sun, visible from England?' In my childish handwriting, I wrote 'August 11th, 1999.' Thirty years earlier, that seemed like the impossibly remote future. Picture, then, my sense of wonder as our family sat on a cliff on England's south coast on that very day, when at exactly the appointed minute, we were plunged into darkness. We expected it, of course, and had gone to see it; but part of the wonder lay in the very fact that it all happened right on time. Predictions like this are possible because of God's ordering of the universe. Weather-forecasting (at least on a limited timescale) is possible. It doesn't rain jelly or snow sherbet. I sow spinach in our garden in the spring, and up it comes in the summer. The tide tables predict the rise and fall of the ocean with astonishing accuracy.

---

6.   See the extra note after chapter 7.

Is this not a mark of God's goodness to us? Who would want to live in a world like that described in Genesis 1:2? Even if the details puzzle us, verse 2 is there to show that such a world can be conceived, and we should not take what we have for granted. Another reason for giving thanks.

This orderliness also makes science possible. We have an expression for the orderly ways of creation: we call them 'the laws of nature'. E does have a habit of equalling mc^2. Hammers dropped off the Empire State Building find a way of accelerating towards Fifth Avenue at 9.81 metres per second for every second they fall. Hence, part of the scientific method: from experiments, you can make generalizations. You can formulate laws and describe the universe mathematically. Indeed, some historians of science have proposed that it was the recognition, derived from the Bible, that God has put order into creation that led some early scientists to look for it. In his book *God's Undertaker,* John Lennox quotes the German astronomer Johannes Kepler, a key figure in the seventeenth-century 'scientific revolution': 'The chief aim of all investigations of the external world should be to discover the rational order which has been imposed on it by God, and which he revealed to us in the language of mathematics.' Lennox goes on to show the connection between a Biblical worldview and the rise of modern science in the sixteenth and seventeenth centuries.[7]

It is very important to note how Genesis so strongly emphasizes the orderliness of creation. For the very fact

---

7.   John Lennox, *God's Undertaker* (Oxford: Lion, 2007), 1st edition, chapter 1.

that the world does behave according to laws has led many, quite wrongly, to conclude there is no room for God. We think we have explained things, so that what we used to think of as God's work is actually explicable by the laws of science. God is left to occupy only the realm of the irregular and the weird, that which can't be 'explained' by science – a realm which, as science progresses, inevitably shrinks. Indeed, much of the 'science-has-replaced-Genesis' story we are so used to hearing is based on the assumption that if we can explain something with scientific laws, this must lead us to deny God's existence – as the businesswoman on the coach thinks. But Genesis thinks differently. By stressing the orderliness of creation, it insists that the very regularity which we observe is *itself* God's work. The 'explainability' of our world is not a sign of God's absence but of his orderliness – more than that, of his goodness to us. Science, far from disproving God, has as its very foundation the fact that God has put law into the universe.

Near where I live in Cambridge, England, is the famous Cavendish Laboratory, where the electron was discovered. Above the front door are inscribed in Latin the words of Psalm 111:2: 'Great are the works of the LORD, studied by all who delight in them.' It is the orderliness of those works which make their study so rewarding and productive.

A remarkable hint about God, the world and us
Here, then, are four great truths about our world; but Genesis 1 also drops a hint about God's plan for us humans, and the way our world should relate to us. It

is only a hint, but it runs right through the passage, and makes a rather surprising point.

The hint comes in the way Genesis 1 is so startlingly selective and slanted in its reporting of the creation. Far from the wide-ranging view of the universe we are used to in modern science (which tells us about everything from black holes to dinosaurs), Genesis focuses only on those aspects of creation which are most directly relevant to us humans, and their relationship to us. Indeed, as the different aspects of the creation are introduced, it is as if they have been made with us in mind. Consider:

- The focus of the account is earth, our home. The formation of the stars is covered so astonishingly briefly: *and the stars* (16).

- When Genesis speaks of the plants (11-12), there is no attempt to classify them as we would (e.g. mosses, grasses, ferns and the rest of a basic botany lesson); we are told only about plants and trees, and that they have seeds and fruits (11-12). The writer is interested mainly in the bits we eat. We might say that he writes from the perspective of a chef, not a botanist!

- When the sun and moon are described (14-18), God says:

  > Let them be for signs and for seasons, and for days and years, and let them be lights in the expanse of the heavens to give light upon the earth. (14-15)

There is not much here to interest astronomers. Genesis seems interested merely in their role as clocks and lights, a huge version of what we buy in the hardware store. It is almost as if they had just been made for us.

- The classification of the land animals (24-25) is into only three kinds: *livestock and creeping things and beasts of the earth*. It is so different from even the most basic mammal-reptile-amphibian (etc.) classification. But again, what seems to matter to Genesis is the animals' connection to us. *Livestock* we raise and live with, *beasts of the earth* we either hunt or avoid, and *creeping things* we tread on. This is a classification of animals not based on size or shape, but how they relate to us.

So Genesis' account of creation is remarkably human-centred, even before we get to the creation of humanity. God separated the land from the sea to give us somewhere to live. He created plants to give us something to eat. The sun and moon light the planet and help us as clocks and calendars. Even the animals can be considered only in relationship to us. It puts an astonishing thought into our minds: could he have created all these in some way for *us*? Are *we* that important in his plans? Were *we* in his mind throughout this process?

We are quick to dismiss Genesis' account as unscientific or lacking sophistication, because it does not classify things as we would, and misses many things out. Where are the dinosaurs? Or the black holes? Or the great distances of space? Indeed, we are often told that Genesis simply reflects a pre-scientific world view, when people were ignorant of much of nature and had not yet developed a proper classification system; it has an earth-centric world view which reflects the values of an age that did not understand the universe. But isn't that to miss the point? The more carefully we read Genesis, the more obvious it becomes that it is being *deliberately selective, because it has a message to tell.* Here it is being deliberately earth-centred to make a point about the privileged place of humanity in God's plans for his creation.

In his book *Pale Blue Dot*, astronomer Carl Sagan wrote how an image of earth taken by the spacecraft *Voyager* from billions of miles away, showing our planet as a tiny point of light in space, should change our view of ourselves. Now that we can see ourselves from so far away, we seem so very insignificant: 'Our planet is a lonely speck in the great enveloping cosmic dark. In our obscurity, in all this vastness, there is no hint that help will come from elsewhere to save us from ourselves.'[8] On the contrary: Genesis 1 carefully and purposefully hints at the opposite conclusion. While it is true that we live in a vast universe, to God we have very great significance.

The idea that God should have made so much in our world with us in his sights should provoke many thoughts. Think about that when you next enjoy walking on the beach, or eating a good meal. Ponder his generosity and his good intentions towards us. Reflect on the significance of human beings in God's eyes. And marvel at this: if he has done all this for us, does this not suggest he has a great purpose for us? Does this not make you want to seek him and know him better and better?

---

8.   Carl Sagan, *Pale Blue Dot* (London: Headline, 1995), p. 9. Sagan does not seem to have spotted that King David made a similar observation many years earlier, but reached a very different conclusion: see Psalm 8:3.

GENESIS 1:26-30

²⁶ Then God said, 'Let us make man in our image, after our likeness. And let them have dominion over the fish of the sea and over the birds of the heavens and over the livestock and over all the earth and over every creeping thing that creeps on the earth.'

²⁷So God created man in his own image,
    in the image of God he created him;
    male and female he created them.

²⁸And God blessed them. And God said to them, 'Be fruitful and multiply and fill the earth and subdue it and have dominion over the fish of the sea and over the birds of the heavens and over every living thing that moves on the earth.' ²⁹And God said, 'Behold, I have given you every plant yielding seed that is on the face of all the earth, and every tree with seed in its fruit. You shall have them for food. ³⁰And to every beast of the earth and to every bird of the heavens and to everything that creeps on the earth, everything that has the breath of life, I have given every green plant for food.' And it was so.

5 Know your place
Genesis 1:26-30

She communicates in sign language, using a vocabulary of over 1,000 words. She also understands spoken English, and often carries on 'bilingual' conversations, responding in signs to questions asked in English. She is learning the letters of the alphabet, and can read some printed words, including her own name. She has achieved scores of between 85 and 95 on the Stanford-Binet Intelligence test.[1]

That's a gorilla called Koko. Apparently, she is also able to make faces, draw representationally and laugh at her own jokes. Chimps are like us too: a random selection of bits of our genome (genetic make-up) reveals over 95 per cent of it to be the same as theirs. So what's the big deal about being human? Are we, as atheist philosopher Peter Singer says, 'speciesist' to claim a special status for the human race?

---

1. Francine Patterson and Wendy Gordon, 'The Case for the Personhood of Gorillas', quoted in Peter Singer, *Rethinking Life and Death* (Oxford: OUP, 1994) p. 181.

Genesis celebrates animals. God made the waters swarm with the creatures of the sea, and filled the skies with the creatures that fly. He made the earth bring forth all the land animals. He blessed them and caused them to multiply, and twice we are told that all this was *good* (1:20-25). We are right to feel something of the Creator's pleasure as we read about all these living things. And yet, as we come to the section from 1:26 onwards describing the creation of humanity, we cannot help noticing that we humans are given a place of unique importance.

Genesis stresses this in various ways. As we have already seen, the description of the non-human creation focuses mainly on its relationship to humanity: the plants are mentioned for their food value, the moon is there as a calendar-keeper, the animals are classified only by the way they relate to *us*. Moreover, the creation of humanity itself (1:26-30) gets more column inches than anything else in the account. In many ways it is a kind of climax: we are God's final creative project. Even the details of the language used about our creation are different. Of the animals, God says, 'Let the earth bring forth living creatures...' (24); of us, God says, as if deliberating, 'Let <u>us</u> make man...' (26).[2] It is as if his direct personal involvement in our creation is specially important – because we are specially important.

Who, then, does Genesis say we are? The answer affects the whole way we think of ourselves, and all sorts of practical areas of life. Let us dig into the account, then consider some implications.

---

2. Whether the 'us' is a kind of 'royal we' or possibly a hint of the Triune person of God is discussed at length in the commentaries. Either way, it is God speaking.

Male and female (1:27)

Male and female he created them. This brief statement in the little bit of poetry in Genesis 1:27 is easy to miss, because it seems such a statement of the obvious. But why should Genesis want to state the obvious? The animals are not described as being male and female, even though they are. It looks as if Genesis is emphasizing that being made male and female is fundamental to our identity as humans. The Creator particularly wanted us to be these two types of person: the same, yet different.

Our gender is right at the root of our being. It's pretty likely that the very first thing anybody said about you or me, at the moment we were born, was whether we were a boy or a girl! By including this note, Genesis makes it sound as if this gender distinctiveness is something the Creator wants us to celebrate, rather than regret or deny. God made men to be men, and women, women. *Vive la différence!* Indeed, since male / female is basic to our humanity, it should not surprise us that it turns out to be a significant theme through the Bible. We will see in due course that Genesis returns to this too.

Made in God's image (1:26-28)

Humanity and the land animals have much in common. Both humans and animals are made on the sixth day. Both are blessed by God. And both are given the commandment, *be fruitful and multiply*. With such similarities in the Genesis account, it should not surprise us that we closely resemble the animals in various ways, as geneticists, zoologists and anthropologists rightly point out. So a chimp's hands are uncannily like ours. Maybe you have a dog – and enjoy teaching it new commands.

But Genesis also draws our attention to a huge difference between humanity and animals. In 1:26 it describes us with a new term, used only of us and never of the animal kingdom. Three times in two verses, we are told that we are made *in the image of God.*

The image – of *God*! Understandably, this striking expression has been the cause of a great deal of discussion. What, exactly, does it mean? At its most basic, it must mean that somehow we resemble God. In verse 26, *in his image* is explained by the phrase that follows, *in his likeness.* The same usage comes in Genesis 5:3, when we are told that *Adam... fathered a son in his own likeness, after his image.* Seth is a chip off the old block. Being in God's image means being a chip off his. (The same two terms have been found, paired, in an Aramaic inscription on a ninth-century B.C. statue in north-east Syria, used as if *likeness* and *image* are parallel.[3])

But in what sense are we similar to God? Over the centuries there has been a great deal of discussion. Some have taken this to mean that we in some sense must be physically similar to God, taking their cue from the fact that in the Old Testament most occurrences of the word *image* have a physical sense.[4] Others have proposed that we resemble God in our great intelligence. Others again have spoken of our religious instinct or a capacity to relate to God – that we are spiritual beings. And so it goes on: a huge amount has been written on the subject (unsurprisingly, because we want to know who we are). But, with all this literature, the danger is that we

---

3.   Collins, *Genesis 1–4*, p. 65.

4.   See Alec Motyer, *Look to the Rock* (Leicester: IVP, 1996), ch. 4, for an account of various aspects of 'the image of God'.

neglect the simple question: what, exactly, does *Genesis itself* mean by *the image of God*? We must take care not to impose our own understandings on the text. While some of these explanations have much truth about them, none of them is where Genesis itself starts.

The clue – as in any passage in the Bible – must lie in the context. Genesis stresses one area of resemblance between us and God, above all others:

> Then God said, 'Let us make man in our image, after our likeness. And let them have dominion over the fish of the sea and over the birds of the heavens and over the livestock and over all the earth and over every creeping thing that creeps on the earth.' (26)

In this verse, being *in the image of God* is closely tied to the idea of ruling. God, as we have already seen, is the ruler of the universe. He has made us as creatures who resemble him in that we share in that rule, too. The human race has been given a kingly status and role. To reinforce the point, the connection between image and rule continues:

> So God created man in his own image,
> in the image of God he created him;
> male and female he created them. (27)
> And God blessed them. And God said to them, 'Be fruitful and multiply and fill the earth and subdue it and have dominion over the fish of the sea and over the birds of the heavens and over every living thing that moves on the earth.' (28)

The pattern of verses 26-28, then, is image-rule-image-rule. The connection is obvious. He is the great Ruler; he has given us ruling authority too. We are in his image in that we have, like him, a kind of kingly status. As Gordon Wenham says, 'The strongest case has been made for the view that the divine image makes man God's vice-regent on earth.'[5] In this respect we are quite different from the animals.

Right from the start, this rule carries with it responsibility. Compare God's blessing of the animals (1:22) with his blessing of humanity (1:28):

> And God blessed them, saying 'Be fruitful and multiply...' (1:22)

> And God blessed them. And God said to them, 'Be fruitful and multiply...' (1:28)

It sounds so similar, but there is a vital difference. Only to the humans God speaks *to them*, personally. His command to the animals is something which, in a sense, they have no choice about. But to humanity, God speaks personally, addressing his command to us as if it is up to us to obey. He is treating us as beings who are responsible for our actions. Of course: you cannot be a ruler without being treated as responsible.

Rule in practice (1:29-30)

Genesis goes on to give an intriguing example of what this rule looks like in practice. In 1:29-30, we can again play 'spot the difference' between two parallel sentences:

> And God said [to humanity] 'Behold, I have given you every plant yielding seed that is on the face of the earth, and every tree with seed in its fruit. You shall have them

---

5. Wenham, *Genesis 1–15,* pp. 31-2. See also D. J. A. Clines' important article 'The image of God in man' (*Tyndale Bulletin* 19 [1968], pp. 53-103), available on the web, which also makes and explains this point.

for food. And to every beast of the earth and to every
bird of the heavens and to everything that creeps on the
earth, everything that has the breath of life, I have given
every green plant for food.' (1:29-30)

Do you see the differences? For one thing, humanity is
again addressed directly, unlike the animals, emphasizing
our responsibility. But another difference concerns
something which at first sight seems mundane and
unimportant: *seeds*. Humanity is given plants *yielding seeds*
and the animals are not. This cannot mean that in some
sense seeds may not be food for animals: very obviously,
they are. I take it that the significance of seeds here is
that they imply agriculture. Animals forage; we normally
farm. This is a simple and rather basic example of the
way we exercise our kingly rule. The animals graze and
hunt; we plough the fields and scatter (even those human
societies which practise hunting and gathering as their
livelihood do so as a purposeful, deliberate adaptation to
a tough local environment, sometimes forced on them
by historical events).

Farming is emblematic of the way we humans control
our environment, in a way quite unlike the animals.
Unlike even Koko, we build cities, irrigate land, mine
metals, put people into space and even alter the entire
global ecosystem. We divert rivers, write symphonies
(some of us), develop information technology and
genetically modify crops. When the newspaper headlines
speak of our 'playing God' – as they have done, when
speaking of breakthroughs in genetic engineering –
they are actually not far off the mark! God has given
us an astonishing degree of ruling authority, and a very

great level of responsibility. So great is this, in fact, that a frightening question springs to mind: what would happen to life if we were to exercise such rule while at the same time rejecting God? But we are getting ahead of ourselves.

Genesis, it turns out, is surprisingly interested in the physical way we exercise our rule over creation: we will see it again in 2:5-6 (irrigation and working the land), 2:15 (looking after the Garden), 3:17-19 (the agonies of cultivating the ground), 4:2 (Cain and Abel's work), 4:17 (building a city), and 4:20-22 (livestock farming, music and technology). We are indeed in the image of God the creating ruler. As the Psalmist says to God, 'You made him [humanity] ruler over the works of your hands; you put everything under his feet.'[6]

Now, of course, our status as rulers is not absolute, but under God's authority. That is clear from the way it is derived from him. As he says: 'Let them have dominion...' (1:26). The command for us to rule is a command from God. We have authority given by God, and under him. We are managers, under the supervision of the chief executive officer; we are not the top of the chain of command. But we still have been given real authority.

It is important to note that in these verses *all* humanity bears the image of God. Male and female are in his image; all people are. Collectively, we are to exercise the responsibility of rule, but this does not mean that there is an ounce less of God's image in an individual who is not top of the tree. No. It is a dignity which each of us bears. Each of us, without exception, belongs to a race which collectively and uniquely has this privilege.

6.   Psalm 8:6, NIV

The tasks God has given us

What are we to do with the kingly responsibility God has given us?

In 1:28 we have the first words spoken by God to humankind in Genesis. There are two elements. First, reproduction in order to populate the planet: 'Be fruitful and multiply and fill the earth'. Second, 'subdue it and have dominion over the fish of the sea and over the birds of the heavens and over every living thing that moves on the earth.' In each case, the language is repetitious and emphatic: *and... and... and*. The writer has his highlighter pen out. These are really important.

The two concepts – reproduction and subduing the world – are linked. There need to be plenty of us if we are to fulfil the Creator's mandate to rule the world effectively. Underlying this is a fascinating assumption: that the natural world needs us as its rulers if it is fully to flourish. Just as the world has been made with us in mind, we have been made with the world in mind; there is a beautiful pattern in which each needs the other.

The word translated *subdue* is a strong word: it is used elsewhere in the Hebrew Bible of military conquest.[7] Our rule is most obviously expressed in the domestication of plants and animals, but extends one way or another to our relationship to all our fellow creatures. The natural world is awesomely good; but it still has to be managed, indeed, subdued. Even though in 1:31 we read that 'God saw everything he had made, and behold, it was very good', that same *very good* world is still assumed to be a world that is wild, and needs taming; indeed,

---

7.   E.g. Numbers 32:29

responsible human rule if it is to function properly. (If, at this point, you are feeling nervous, because the words *rule* and *subdue* conjure up images of environmental tyranny, wait for the extra note at the end of the chapter.)

An English vicar was once riding his bike through the village, and saw one of his parishioners at work in his garden. As the vicar admired the flowers, a pious thought welled up. 'Ah,' he said, 'how wonderful are the works of God!' The gardener replied, 'Actually, Vicar, it was quite a lot of my work too!' Perhaps he had half an eye for the vicar's garden, which hadn't seen much attention in ages! God has made the world to need humanity as its ruler. Just as the world has been made for us, we have been made for it. God intended humanity to be the linchpin of the global ecosystem.[8]

Two direct and personal applications follow from these verses. First, let's be positive about having children, if we are able to do so. It's God's will that we should *be fruitful and multiply* – for the planet needs ruling. That is not to say that we must have massive families – indeed, there are some parts of the world where overpopulation is clearly a challenge – or that birth-control is intrinsically wrong. But we probably do need to be much more positive about having children than our selfish Western society often is (in some European countries, reproduction is actually below the rate which replaces the population). Christians, it's good to say, still believe in having children: witness the people-carriers in the car parks at some Christian conventions!

Secondly, let's be positive about work. It is basic to our existence, as God has given it to us. The so-called

---

8. See ahead to Genesis 2:5-6 for an example of how the land needs man if it is to flourish.

Protestant work ethic is, in fact, a Biblical ethic, starting here in Genesis. For sure, as we will see in Genesis 3, a consequence of sin is that work has been twisted into grind and toil, but here we see that work itself is God's good plan, right from the beginning. In working, we should be making a contribution to the good of the world, and to each other; it is, collectively, how we exercise our rule. Unemployment is a great sadness, because it denies people the opportunity to exercise this God-given role.

The responsibility that goes with being human

There is a further, and vitally important, implication for us from what Genesis says about humanity's unique position. It is that taking responsibility for our lives, and our world, is at the very heart of what it means to be human. God says *Rule...* and this means, on the day-to-day level, that we are to take responsibility for our lives, as our share in taking responsibility for the world around us.

Of course, at a personal level, our responsibilities vary. Adults have greater responsibilities than children, and some people, for various reasons, are not able to take responsibility for much. It is vital that we remember that this does not make them for one minute any the less human; rather, because we are all human it becomes the responsibility of the rest of us to care for, love and protect them. But, this said, each of us does need to take hold of the particular tasks and duties God has given us in life, whether great or small. All parents will know that their great aim in parenting is to help their children grow up to take responsibility for themselves.

Do you, like me, need to hear this? Throughout life we are tempted to shirk our responsibilities, for our families, for our work and for our own lives. We run away from things; we do not face up to problems; we procrastinate; we pass the buck; we are careless. I admit that I have sometimes looked at our cat, and envied his lack of responsibility, as he lies curled up on the rug! But to run away from the responsibilities God has set before us is actually to deny the unique and privileged role God has given us as those made in his image.

Genesis 3 will go on to show us that the first casualty of rebellion against God is evasion of responsibility: 'It wasn't my fault!'[9] We are made in the image of God, to rule the world, under his authority. Ask this question today: What responsibilities have I been given that I need to face up to? In what way must I exercise my God-given role of ruling? Asking that question is being authentically human – and altogether different from Koko the gorilla.

EXTRA NOTE: A LICENCE FOR EXPLOITATION?

The sad reality of much human rule of the world is often one which results in extinction of species, loss of habitats, pollution, flooding and even climate change. Can part of the blame be attached to an arrogance deriving from Genesis' teaching about human rule? In a highly influential article in 1967, historian of science Lynn White argued this. He wrote, 'Both our present science and our present technology are so tinctured with orthodox Christian arrogance toward nature that no solution for our ecological crisis can be expected from them alone ... Since the roots of our trouble are largely religious, the remedy must be religious, whether we call it

---

9.   Genesis 3:12

that or not.'[10] He went on to advocate a 'Franciscan' view of nature, which in his view sees all nature as equal.

But Genesis must be allowed to speak for itself, and the answer is simple. *Rule* is not the same as *exploitation*. In the Garden, as we will go on to see in chapter 2, the man is to exercise a duty of care, looking after or guarding it (2:15). Further, Noah (Genesis 6), who clearly exercises rule over animals, is an arch-conservationist! *Rule* does not imply ruling badly. In fact, we know the solution is not neglect, but ruling well: it is striking that every environmental action scheme we ever hear about starts with something *we* should do. The creation of a national park is just as much an act of rule as chopping down trees.

At a more profound level, Genesis itself, in chapter 3, will go on to show us that the problem lies not in the concept of human rule as such, but in *the nature of the ruler*. The problem comes from the fact that we have rebelled against God, as a result of which our rule is both frustrated and distorted. Responsible stewardship has been replaced by senseless exploitation, and a toxic mixture of tyranny, abdication and loss of control. That is the ultimate fact behind every man-made environmental disaster. And this is why we are so nervous whenever we hear talk of rule: the ruler is, in fact, a tyrant! Unavoidably, we read Genesis 1 from the perspective of a Genesis 3 world.

Genesis will point to our problems being solved, neither by being embarrassed about our rule over the natural world, nor by encouraging us to abandon it, but by God himself dealing with the state of the ruler. That is God's great project – and the theme of the whole of the Bible.

---

10. Lynn Townsend White, Jr, 'The Historical Roots of Our Ecologic Crisis', *Science*, Vol. 155 (1967), pp. 1203-7; quote from final paragraph.

One of the biggest questions we face is 'if there is a God, why is the world in such a mess?' A large part of the answer will come in Genesis 3. But already, here in Genesis 1, the case is being opened, and we are beginning to see who the chief suspect must be. Once we know that, is it only the stuff of dreams to say that when the problem surrounding him is sorted, the world will rejoice in his rule? The Apostle Paul looked forward to that as a certainty:

> For the creation waits with eager longing for the revealing of the sons of God.[11]

---

11.   Romans 8:19

6

More on the 'image'

Genesis 1:26-30
and the rest of the Bible

The rest of the Bible brings out some momentous implications that follow from our being *in the image of God*. In this chapter, we will travel beyond Genesis 1 to take a brief sample of five truths that follow from this claim, each either specifically stated or implied in Scripture.

The unique preciousness of human life

'Once you dehumanize people, you can do anything to them.' It was the summer of 2011, and a Libyan, being interviewed on radio, was explaining how the crumbling regime of Colonel Muammar Gaddafi was encouraging its supporters to commit atrocities against the opposition. He said that the government made a point of calling its opponents 'rats'.

As I listened, I found myself pondering the interviewee's unstated assumption – that a human being has a value altogether different from an animal. It is, of course, a very Genesis-like way of thinking, and comes up in the first reference to God's image after the initial creation account. In Genesis 9:6, set after the great flood, God is talking about humanity's relationship with animals. Life, symbolized by a creature's blood, is precious; but human life is more precious yet. Murder is a most serious offence, and to highlight that, Genesis breaks from prose to verse just for a single sentence:

> 'Whoever sheds the blood of man,
> by man shall his blood be shed,
> for God made man in his own image.'

One could hardly state the value of human life more strongly. It stems from our being in God's image. Murder is more than merely the killing of a body; it is taking the life of one whom God has made to resemble himself.

As well as the obvious wickedness of murder as normally defined, this same principle underlies Christian grief over abortion, infanticide and euthanasia. Christians are always going to be awkward customers when discussing these things: when the easy-going, sensible-sounding utilitarian says 'it is the best thing to do in the circumstances,' we can only reply that there is an intrinsic preciousness to human beings, stemming from our God's-image status. Of course, it sounds awkward but, as history has shown so often, we deny it at our peril. What answer has a merely utilitarian view of human life and death got to the ethics of the Third Reich?

If Western culture still upholds the unique value of human life, that is in large part because over the centuries it has been marinated in the Bible. But we should not take it for granted. There are other ways of thinking. In his book *Rethinking Life and Death*,[1] Peter Singer, Professor of Bioethics at Princeton (and widely acknowledged as the inventor of 'animal liberation'), has charted a course for those who deny that we are made in the image of God. Singer, an atheist, assumes that the Biblical view has been superseded (he does not say why). He accepts that humans have value, but argues that we differ from 'non-human animals' only in degree, not kind. A healthy deer caught in a trap might deserve our attempts to rescue it more than a baby with severe defects. Animal rights should be promoted, and human euthanasia encouraged. There is no overarching reason for treating humans entirely differently. He speaks sympathetically of those societies which have practised infanticide.

In a sense, Singer's views are consistent. If you do not believe in God, why believe in the image of God? If you do not believe humans have this unique status, why should they be treated differently from 'non-human animals'? It has been said wisely that if you abolish God, you end up abolishing man.

Interestingly, Singer's lecture tours have sometimes been dogged by protesters, often from groups representing disabled people. Even if they have wrongly assumed that Singer goes further than he does, their nervousness is understandable – for they are simply thinking through the possible implications of his position.

What a relief the Genesis worldview is! Restating it clearly and publicly in a society drifting towards a survival-of-the-most-useful ethic may mean the saving of many lives.

---

1. Peter Singer, *Rethinking Life and Death: The Collapse of our Traditional Ethics* (Oxford: OUP, 1994).

The importance of respecting everyone

The Apostle James also picks up the language of being made in God's image. He is writing about the need to control our tongues, and complains of our personal inconsistency in using them: 'With it we bless our Lord and Father, and with it we curse people who are made in the likeness of God.'[2] Here is the church guitarist who loves to lead the band at Sunday church, but insults the ref at his son's school football match on Saturday. Here is the person who prays to God on Sunday but preys on his neighbour the rest of the week! It is strange, James argues, to be all pious before God but then curse those he has made to be like him.

The principle behind what James says is one of proper respect for all our fellow human beings, whoever they are. That includes the ref at the match, or whoever else we may be tempted to demonize – politicians, bankers, traffic wardens or whoever (and I must not go on, lest I pander to my own prejudices!). It means saying no to all forms of racism, and it is no coincidence that Wilberforce and many of those who campaigned against the wickedness of the African slave trade two hundred years ago were steeped in a Biblical worldview. It means saying no to snobbery, or even to the foolish ageism which has infected Western culture and which values the young more highly than the old. It means listening to people, paying them the respect (without being naive) of taking them at their word, and seeking to promote their welfare.

Recognizing that all people are made in God's image will make us treat them with a proper dignity. I heard of

---

2.   James 3:9

a homeless man who received friendship and practical help from a Christian. He asked the Christian, 'Why do you bother with me?' 'Because you are made in the image of God', came the reply. Think about that, as you survey a world of need.

Accountability

There is a less comfortable consequence of our being in God's image. A great theme of the Bible is that God treats humanity as responsible for our actions. From the moment in Genesis 3 when God confronts the first human pair, to the last judgment at the end of time, God requires an accounting. He does, and will, judge us. Although the Bible does not explicitly link this with being in God's image, its root is here in Genesis, for it is a direct entailment of being given responsibility for our lives and our world. Responsibility must mean accountability. In his 1949 essay 'The humanitarian theory of punishment', C. S. Lewis argued against an increasingly popular view of criminal justice which sought to use the law's sanctions only to 'cure' offenders or to act as a deterrent. He made the point that only when we treat people according to what they *deserve* – even when it means punishing them – are we really giving them their full human dignity, because only then are we treating them as fully responsible. Lewis writes:

> To be 'cured' against one's will and cured of states which we may not regard as disease is to be put on a level with those who have not yet reached the age of reason or those who never will; to be classed with infants, imbeciles, and domestic animals. But to be

punished, however severely, because we have deserved it, because 'we ought to have known better', is to be treated as a human person made in God's image.[3]

In his magnificent book *The Cross of Christ*, John Stott applies this same Biblical way of thinking to God's relationship with us. He explains 'the problem of forgiveness' and shows what our human responsibility must inevitably lead to:

> Our responsibility before God is an inalienable aspect of our human dignity. Its final expression will be on the day of judgment. Nobody will be sentenced without trial. All people, great and small, irrespective of their social class, will stand before God's throne, not crushed or browbeaten, but given this final token of respect for human responsibility, as each gives an account of what he or she has done.[4]

We may find the idea of God's judgment hard to take, and some are outraged by the suggestion that he might punish anyone at all. But his doing this is a natural consequence, not only of his perfect justice, but also of the dignity he has given us as responsible beings. He who made us in his image takes our actions with the utmost seriousness. Each must give an account; which is why it is vital that we discover where, alone, his forgiveness is to be found.

Where to get an idea of what God is like

There is a further, and quite different, consequence of our being *in the image of God*. God is invisible; how can we

---

3. C. S. Lewis, 'The humanitarian theory of punishment' (*Australian Quarterly Review 3*, 1949, 5-12); widely available on the web.

4. John Stott, *The Cross of Christ*, pp. 95-6.

know what he is like? Creation, of course, gives us many clues: he is brilliant, powerful and majestic beyond our imagining. But there is another clue. It is we ourselves. We are made like him. We are in his image.

Religion down the ages has often had at its heart the practice of making images of the relevant god or gods: a statue, a painting, an object which is worshipped. The idea is to help us visualize the deity or deities and help us in our veneration. But one of the great distinctives of Biblical religion is that this practice is completely banned. The second commandment famously says,

> 'You shall not make for yourself a carved image, or any likeness of anything that is in heaven above, or that is in the earth beneath, or that is in the water under the earth. You shall not bow down to them or serve them, for I the LORD your God am a jealous God...'[5]

Why? Because the true God is, of course, living, active, sovereign and glorious. It is absurd, insulting and inevitably misleading to represent him with a lifeless statue. Moreover, the true God is our creator; we are getting things entirely the wrong way round if we think we can create him!

But does that mean we have no image of God in terms that we could relate to? No. He has provided an image of his own. *We* are in God's image: we bear his mark. If you want to see the entity that most closely resembles God in our world, you have only to look in the mirror! That sounds extraordinarily pretentious, but it is a simple implication of being in his image. Again, that does not necessarily imply a physical resemblance,

---

5. Exodus 20:4-5

but it does remind us that God is a person, not a force; and living, active, powerful, ruling – as we are.

This is important. If we resemble God, then he cannot be what some people call 'wholly Other', in other words, so completely different from us that we cannot understand him, communicate with him, or he with us. For he and us to talk together is not like an elephant trying to talk to an ant, or aliens from different universes trying to enjoy a cup of coffee. God can communicate with us, using human words. Do not let anyone tell you that God is so far beyond our ken that he must remain a mystery. We happen to have been made in his image.

And yet, of course, there is a problem: we have become sinful, as Genesis will soon explain. We have habits of heart and attitudes of mind that are altogether different from God's, and we do things that are quite foreign to his nature. As a result of this, our rule over the world is a very poor reflection of God's rule, and we are a dreadful guide to his character. So where can we go to see what God really looks like in terms we can understand, and yet which is totally reliable? The answer comes in another of the places in the Bible where the *image* theme recurs. Paul wrote to the church in Colossae: 'He is the image of the invisible God, the firstborn of all creation.'[6] There was once, just once, a man who throughout his life was (and remains) *the* perfect image of God: the Carpenter from Nazareth.

Here is a man – in God's image. Because people are in the image of God, for the Son of God to become one of us was an entirely fitting (though huge!) step. And when we look at him we really see just what God is like.

6. Colossians 1:15

If we want to know God, here is the place to go! We need go no further, and indeed can go no further. In Christ, *the* image of the invisible God, God has made himself known perfectly.

Value

Being made in God's image also underlines our own personal value in God's eyes. On the first evening of a church course introducing the Christian faith, we ask everyone to write down the one question they would ask God if they could. One person wrote this question to God: *I appreciate how intricate and amazing our world is and I believe in you, but I cannot understand my purpose in your grand scheme of things. I feel insignificant in life and world.* Genesis 1 is the obvious place to turn for the answer: it so clearly shows that in his eyes, we matter very, very much.

GENESIS 1:31–2:3

[31]And God saw everything that he had made, and behold, it was very good. And there was evening and there was morning, the sixth day.

[2:1]Thus the heavens and the earth were finished, and all the host of them. [2]And on the seventh day God finished his work that he had done, and he rested on the seventh day from all his work that he had done. [3]So God blessed the seventh day and made it holy, because on it God rested from all his work that he had done in creation.

7 The finished work and the seventh day

Genesis 1:31–2:3

A *seventh* day? On the face of things, there is no need for it. If ever there were a concluding sentence, surely it is this: 'And God saw everything that he had made, and behold, it was very good' (1:31). So aren't we done by now? It feels like the right place to stop, and certainly those responsible for the chapter division of our Bibles (in the Middle Ages) thought so. They drew the line between chapters at the end of the sixth day, and left the seventh strangely isolated, in a new chapter. It does look like a curious addition.

Until, that is, we remember that *seven* has been on the cards since the beginning. We have already seen the way the writer loves the number seven, with a seven-word opening sentence (1:1), seven uses of the expression *And God saw that it was good*, fourteen mentions of God's speech, thirty-five mentions of his name, and other excursions into the seven-times table. Thus, we are drawn towards this seventh day as if towards a summit, with the number series *first*, *second*, *third*.... increasing our anticipation. The creation of humanity on the sixth day has been a kind of climax, but now Genesis climbs beyond that.

So why the seventh day, and why is it drawn to our attention? It is not as if God needed a rest. It is impossible to imagine the all-mighty Maker of heaven and earth running out of steam, drooping, putting on his slippers. Nor, from one point of view, is his work actually over: as Jesus said, 'My Father is working until now, and I am working.'[1] There must be some very good reasons why the seventh day is emphasized as it is.

God the finisher

The most striking point in this section is surprisingly often missed. Our tendency is to rush into discussions about the Sabbath (Is it Saturday or Sunday? Should we work? Is it binding on us?), but in the process we forget that Genesis so far has been keen to introduce us, first and foremost, to God himself. So it is much better to ask what this section tells us *about him*.

Just this: he finishes his work. Perhaps we consider this too obvious to deserve our attention, but Genesis presses the point. *Finished* comes in both 2:1 and 2:2. The word translated *rested* in both 2:2 and 2:3 also means *ceased*; the *rest* involved is the kind you take when you sit down after finishing a task. All this is prefaced by 1:31, which has a sense of completeness too: 'And God saw *everything* that he had made'. Job done! The work of creating has now been accomplished, and the stage is set for the events which will unfold in the Garden and beyond.

The fact that God is a finisher of his work is, in part, just re-emphasizing his awesome power. He has all that it takes to see the work right through to its completion. By contrast, we are all familiar with projects which aren't finished,

1. John 5:17

because the instigator lacked the resources to complete them. It makes me think of a scene along the road from our old house. Just visible through the grass and nettles are the outlines of three houses, with just their foundations and concrete floors. I don't know the sad story, but clearly someone, years ago, tried to build them, and something went wrong. Maybe the developer ran out of money, or there was some ugly dispute. The foundations remain as a monument to an unfulfilled dream. But Genesis wants us to know that it is not so with God: he has the power to see the great project of creation right through, and does just that. He is more like my father, who is a marvellous finisher of work: I have never yet seen him leave a home improvement or garden project unfinished.

Of course, in one sense God's work in the natural world is not finished: he makes the sun rise and sends the rain,[2] gives water and food to animals[3] and even continues to push London and New York apart at an inch a year! In every beautiful sunset we marvel at the work of the Creator, who is constantly involved in his world. So what does Genesis mean by saying God *finished*? Theologians helpfully distinguish between God's *creation* and his *providence*. Providence is his ongoing work in the world, in all sorts of ways; as far as the physical world is concerned, this work of his can normally be described by what we call the laws of nature. Creation, on the other hand, is his original work, ultimately from nothing; it includes the establishment of those laws. While there is an overlap between the two, Genesis 1:31 is concerned

---

2. Matthew 5:45

3. Psalm 104:11, 28

with creation. It is also stressing at this point that all that God needed to do to set the stage for the events of chapters 2–3 was by now complete.

Why does Genesis emphasize so strongly that God is a finisher of his work? The answer must be that this great truth underpins some of the Bible's most important teaching about God. In Genesis 12, with the call of Abraham, he will be introduced to us as the one who makes promises: a great distinctive of the God of the Bible. The rest of Genesis then begins to show the keeping of those promises; indeed, it is no exaggeration to say that the pattern of promise and fulfilment ties together the whole story of the Bible. Indeed, his astonishing ability to keep his promises identifies Israel's Lord as the true God, the one who is really there, in contrast to the pagan deities who cannot make anything happen.[4] Here in Genesis 2, we have the foundation of all this: it is the Creator God's characteristic to finish his work.

This should make us lift our heads in hope. For we live in a world which, once again, awaits the completion of God's work. In Genesis 3, we will see the rebellion in the Garden and its disastrous consequences. People are now alienated from God and sinful in heart; the creation is now spoilt. Knowing that God delights in finishing his work (and in his work being finished) means, then, that it should not surprise us that God did not long tolerate this situation. Instead, and as early as Genesis 12, he starts a great plan to put the world back to rights. He promises through the prophets that he will send a great rescuer into the world.

Since God is a finisher of his work, it should not surprise us, either, that he followed through on those

4.   Isaiah 44:6-28

promises and sent Jesus, the promised Rescuer, who fulfilled all that had been prophesied of him, and who, by his death on the cross, did everything necessary to bring rebels, far from God, forgiveness and friendship with their Creator – crying, as he did so, 'It is finished!'[5] Nor should it surprise us that the result of what Jesus did for us on the cross has been astonishingly effective, and that today there are hundreds of millions all over the world who have indeed discovered friendship with God through him. And since God is a finisher of his work, this will culminate in the final removal of all that spoils his world, and the creation of 'new heavens and a new earth'.[6] Sin will be removed, and so will suffering.

Just as the very first verse of Genesis showed us that history had a beginning, so the last verse of this great opening section of the book (2:3) shows that God is a finisher. The seventh day gives us confidence that, just as God finished the work of creation, he will finish the work of saving the world. It is surely significant that when we get to the New Testament book of Hebrews, the writer uses the language of the seventh day to describe the great final future which God promises his people: 'So then, there remains a Sabbath rest for the people of God...'[7]

We are, of course, getting far ahead of ourselves in the story. But we are right to. For even though Genesis 1–2 speaks of the world before the catastrophe of sin, it was written in a world already spoilt by that, for people longing for an answer – as we do. Not a verse of it is merely theoretical, or for our interest alone; it is thoroughly

---

5.   John 19:30

6.   2 Peter 3:13

7.   Hebrews 4:9

practical, pointing us from the beginning towards trusting in our all-sufficient God. And just as, even in 1:2, Genesis hinted that God specializes in creating order from chaos, so again here it gives us ground to trust him as the one who always finishes his work.

Hold on to that! If you are a Christian, you have pinned your life on God's promises about the life of the world to come. As we look around us, there is much to make us weary, and wonder if the promised new heavens and earth will ever come. Will we really meet the multitude of Christ's people that no one could number?[8] Will Jesus really wipe away every tear? Can it be true that one day, death shall be no more?[9] Consider the seventh day, and the God we meet there. He is the one who finishes his work. Just as he finished then, he will finish in future. He will finish his work in us,[10] he will keep all his promises. It's in his nature.

The pattern of the week
We take it for granted that our weeks are seven days long, but they need not be. Why not eight, or six, or five? In fact, in a weird social experiment in 1929, Russia started observing a five-day week – which it managed to sustain until 1940, when it rediscovered seven days! Although it has not been proved, it is thought by many that the universal pattern of a seven-day week derives ultimately from this passage in the Bible and its subsequent influence throughout civilization. The English names of the days of the week may be pagan (Woden's day, Thor's day,

---

8. Revelation 7:9

9. Revelation 21:4

10. Philippians 1:6

etc.), but the shape of the week is biblical. I wonder how many people realise that this pervasive feature of global culture may well derive from the pattern described here?

Genesis 2:3 sets apart the seventh day as *holy*, because on it God rested from his work. The Hebrew word for *rested* or *ceased* is *shavat*, which is related to the word *shabbat*, or Sabbath. Now we see for sure why Genesis emphasizes the days of creation: they are a pattern for the first Hebrew readers of Genesis, who are to hallow the seventh day as special. God's working pattern is to be ours.

The connection is made explicitly in the fourth of the Ten Commandments in the book of Exodus:

> 'Remember the Sabbath day, to keep it holy. Six days you shall labour, and do all your work, but the seventh day is a Sabbath to the LORD your God. On it you shall not do any work, you, or your son, or your daughter, your male servant, or your female servant, or your livestock, or the sojourner who is within your gates.
>
> For in six days the LORD made heaven and earth, the sea, and all that is in them, and rested the seventh day. Therefore the LORD blessed the Sabbath day and made it holy.'[11]

Every seven days, all Israel was to down tools, following this pattern. It was a weekly reminder that there is more to life than work, and, more specifically, that they depended on their Lord for their life and for their existence as his people. Having to take time out, even during the harvest, was an exercise in trust, and a vivid way for them to keep discovering God's provision. And

---

11.   Exodus 20:8-11

every seven days they were also reminded that their God is a finisher of his work; that his great purposes in the world will one day reach their conclusion – indeed, when the Sabbath commandment is repeated in the book of Deuteronomy, it is specifically linked to God's redemption of his people.[12] All this was further reinforced through a system of jubilee and sabbatical years, in addition to the seventh day. Sabbath observance was a badge of Israelite identity as the LORD's nation.

When we get to the New Testament, twice we have hints (though only hints) that some early Christians, where they were able to, gave special attention, not to the seventh, but to the first day of the week (Sunday), because on that day (as on the original first day) a *new* creation began, as Jesus was raised from the dead; this may well have been what was meant by 'the Lord's Day'.[13] They looked forward, as we have seen, to the final rest. Since then, it has been widespread Christian practice (in many of those nations with a seven-day week) to use that day for our equivalent of what ancient Israel called its 'sacred assemblies' – to meet together and hear God's Word.

Does the fourth commandment mean that Sabbath observance remains obligatory today, as our present moral duty? At this point, Bible-believing Christians take differing views. Some argue that since the commandment looks back to creation, that is, before the establishment of the nation of Israel, the requirement to observe a weekly Sabbath is to be obeyed by all, for all time. Others, however, point out that this commandment is the only

---

12. Deuteronomy 5:12-15

13. Acts 20:7; Revelation 1:10

one of the Ten Commandments not specifically reiterated in the New Testament, and that the Apostle Paul does not insist on Sabbath observance; it is fulfilled in Christ.[14] They conclude, therefore, that we now have freedom in this area. Based on these arguments, this second view is my judgment, also.[15]

Jesus, often in controversy about the Sabbath, did not argue from the national, legal requirements of the Sabbath commandment in Exodus, but referred to the Creator's gift in the Sabbath's very inception, saying that 'the Sabbath was made for man.'[16] We have already seen, in Genesis 1, hints of how the Creator designed the world with us in mind; in Genesis 2, we will see God's sheer generosity and goodness further emphasized. Jesus is fitting Sabbath into this context: in blessing the seventh day, God was acting for our good.

This means there is a real personal value in observing a weekly day of rest – surely for most of us best enjoyed on the day we meet as church. Speaking personally, I know that I am easily caught up in life's ceaseless cogs, so I'm very thankful that Genesis' legacy lives on sufficiently in our society to make it possible to take a day off in seven. I can rest that day, trusting that God will meet my needs, and have the joy of meeting with God's people for our mutual

---

14. See Romans 14:5-6 and Colossians 2:16

15. There is obviously a great deal more to say, but in this book we must stick to Genesis! The reader is directed to the literature. For the first view, that Sabbath observance remains a matter of legal obligation, see Joseph A. Pipa, Jr, *The Lord's Day* (Tain: Christian Focus, 2008) and J. I. Packer 'The Puritans and the Lord's Day' in his book *Among God's Giants* (Eastbourne: Kingsway, 1991), pp. 309-23. For the second, see Michael S. Horton *The Law of Perfect Freedom* (Chicago: Moody, 1993), pp. 113-31 and D. A. Carson (ed.) *From Sabbath to Lord's Day* (Grand Rapids: Zondervan, 1982).

16. Mark 2:27

encouragement and strengthening. This is a real 'means of grace', given by God for our blessing. I have pinned my hopes on the God who finishes his work, and am looking forward to that great completion, but I can easily lose sight of that further horizon as the waves of life roll in. I need a weekly rest, and also a reminder that God is *the finisher who will finish*. I doubt you are made differently.

EXTRA NOTE: UNDERSTANDING THE DAYS

The days of creation are such a prominent feature of Genesis 1 that it is reasonable to ask: what exactly are they? If they are understood to be periods of 24 hours, then there is an obvious problem correlating this with the 4.5+ billion years currently estimated as the age of the earth based on radiometric dating – not to mention the considerably greater age proposed for the universe itself. Again and again, in school textbooks, TV documentaries and even academic history books, we are told that people used to believe the Genesis account of origins, namely that the world was formed very quickly and recently; now science has shown it to be of great age. So Genesis must be wrong; a primitive 'myth' happily dispelled by the certainties of science! There has been significant discussion of this for over two hundred years – at least since the father of modern geology, James Hutton, wrote his *Theory of the Earth* in 1785. A furious debate continues to rage, stoked on the one hand by atheists wishing to disprove Christianity, and on the other by some Christians who say the earth scientists have got their timescale wrong.

In this kind of matter we will be wise to speak provisionally, and I state my own view with caution, with the request that you do not disregard the rest of this book if at this point you disagree!

We must start by saying that so great is the Lord revealed to us in Genesis, and so mighty in power, that we should surely

---

have no trouble believing that he could indeed have brought everything we know and see into existence in a very short time. He could have done it in a nanosecond. We must also take the text of Genesis seriously. And it cannot be avoided that, although the Hebrew word *yom* (day) can cover a whole period of time, as in Genesis 2:4, the word in chapter one has its usual meaning, emphasized by the formula 'God called the light Day, and the darkness he called Night' (1:5).

But there is something else which deserves our attention. It is not until the fourth day of creation that the sun and moon are made. These are explicitly there 'to separate the day from the night... for days and years' (1:14). This means that three days have gone by which cannot be 'earth days' in the sense in which we experience them. For when is a day not a day? When there's no sun. Given the care the writer takes with detail, this cannot have escaped his attention, and suggests that the days may not be earth days. (To this we might add that, if we try fitting the account of the creation of man in Genesis 2 with that in Genesis 1, a lot of time seems to have to be fitted into the sixth day – the term *at last* in 2:23 would normally be taken as implying a significant period of time.[17])

What sort of days, then? One school of thought has it that the 'days' are a literary device used for showing how orderly God is in doing his work. It has often been pointed out that there is a deliberate pattern, in which the elements of the first trio of days are filled in, respectively, in the second trio:

1st day: light	4th day: sun, moon and stars
2nd day: sky and waters	5th day: birds and fish
3rd day: land and land plants	6th day: land animals and humanity

---

17. See C. J. Collins, *Science and Faith: Friends or Foes?* (Wheaton, IL: Crossway, 2003), ch. 5.

This structure is clearly there, and I hope we have enough culture about us to let the writer arrange his material like this without accusing him of untruth! We have already seen that Genesis 1 is written in a very stylized way, as almost a kind of prose poem, and that the account is deliberately shaped to stress the importance of man in God's purposes. We do need to take that seriously. This view stems from reverent observation of the text, not trying to avoid it. At least one clear purpose of the highly orderered nature of the passage is that it is emphasizing, by its style, the highly ordered nature of the creation God has made.

But recognizing the literary artistry of the text does not mean we must dismiss any sense of real chronology. Indeed, the book of Exodus does seem to understand the days as actual days. As we have seen, the fourth of the Ten Commandments is about keeping the Sabbath, and gives this reason: 'For in six days the LORD made heaven and earth, the sea, and all that is in them, and rested the seventh day.'[18] A pattern can only be followed if it is in some sense real.

But what were those days? If they are not earth days, can they not be God's days? The passage describes God's own activity, before any human observer. It is wise to point out that the Psalmist tells God that 'a thousand years in your sight are but as yesterday' [same Hebrew word for 'day' as Genesis 1] 'when it is past, or as a watch in the night.'[19] His days are not our days. As T. Desmond Alexander comments: 'By a simple reading of Genesis, these days must be described as days in the life of God, but how these days relate to human days is more difficult to determine.'[20] Genesis, then, could be telling us how God, on the timescale of his days, made the world, setting all its laws, processes and features in place. Beyond this, it seems only wise to leave the question of what, exactly, a day for the LORD looks like, and how this relates to the timescale revealed by

---

18. Exodus 20:11

19. Psalm 90:4

20. T. Desmond Alexander, article 'Genesis' in Lane T. Dennis, ed, *The ESV Study Bible* (Wheaton: Crossway, 2008), p. 50.

geology (both in duration and in sequence[21]), as a matter for the Author of time himself, whose days are beyond our ken.

There are also other possibilities.[22] Whichever of these views turns out to be correct, I believe that they indicate that (assuming the science is correct) there need not necessarily be a conflict between Genesis and current scientific understanding at this point.[23]

One final question. We have now surveyed the themes of Genesis 1, and the main thrust of the passage is obvious. We are introduced to God in all his majesty and power. We learn about the creation: that it is orderly, dependent and good. And Genesis shows us ourselves, made in God's image as his vice-regents. The days have been spelt out, leading up to the climax of the seventh, to impress on us that God is a finisher of his work. Given that this is its big picture message, why should Genesis be concerned to tell us how old the world is?

---

21. See Job 38:4-7, which is also a call for humility in us all!

22. For instance, Alan Hayward's 'Days of fiat' approach, outlined along with other options in *Creation and Evolution: The Facts and the Fallacies* (London: Triangle, 1985), chapter 10; see also John Lennox, *Seven Days that Divide the World* (Grand Rapids: Zondervan, 2011).

23. This treatment is, of course, superficial in relation to the vast literature on the subject. For various versions of the view that the days are a literary device, see Henri Blocher *In the Beginning* (Leicester, IVP, 1984) and the commentaries by Hamilton, Waltke and Wenham. Kidner's commentary has a helpful (typically concise) additional note on this. C. John Collins gives another overview of possibilities, together with his own proposal, both in his commentary and in *Science and Faith* (cited above). See also V. Poythress, *Redeeming Science* (Wheaton, Crossway, 2006), and John Lennox, *Seven Days that Divide the World* (Grand Rapids, Eerdmans, 2011). There are some useful contributions from different standpoints on the 'be thinking' website run by UCCF in the UK: www.bethinking.org.

GENESIS 2:4-17

⁴These are the generations
of the heavens and the earth when they were created,
in the day that the LORD God made the earth and the heavens.

⁵When no bush of the field was yet in the land and no small plant of the field had yet sprung up—for the LORD God had not caused it to rain on the land, and there was no man to work the ground, ⁶and a mist was going up from the land and was watering the whole face of the ground— ⁷then the LORD God formed the man of dust from the ground and breathed into his nostrils the breath of life, and the man became a living creature. ⁸And the LORD God planted a garden in Eden, in the east, and there he put the man whom he had formed. ⁹And out of the ground the LORD God made to spring up every tree that is pleasant to the sight and good for food. The tree of life was in the midst of the garden, and the tree of the knowledge of good and evil.

¹⁰A river flowed out of Eden to water the garden, and there it divided and became four rivers. ¹¹The name of the first is the Pishon. It is the one that flowed around the whole land of Havilah, where there is gold. ¹²And the gold of that land is good; bdellium and onyx stone are there. ¹³The name of the second river is the Gihon. It is the one that flowed around the whole land of Cush. ¹⁴And the name of the third river is the Tigris, which flows east of Assyria. And the fourth river is the Euphrates.

¹⁵The LORD God took the man and put him in the garden of Eden to work it and keep it. ¹⁶And the LORD God commanded the man, saying, 'You may surely eat of every tree of the garden, ¹⁷but of the tree of the knowledge of good and evil you shall not eat, for in the day that you eat of it you shall surely die.'

8 The secret of flourishing
Genesis 2:4-17

There is a beautiful clarity about the way Genesis sequences its topics. We have been introduced to God, and the world he has made; next, we were introduced to humanity. It makes perfect sense, therefore, that Genesis now addresses how God and we *relate to each other* in the world he has made. What are the terms of our relationship? What are his intentions towards us? What does he require of us? This is the clear theme of this section.

At this point, Genesis does a Google Earth®. Users of that software will know how it zooms in, when you launch it, from the whole planet to a particular location somewhere on earth. The Hebrew word for *the earth* can also mean *land*, and this seems to be the sense here. So far, Genesis has given us the global view, but now it takes us to part of the ancient Near East, to a land near the rivers Tigris and Euphrates (2:14). We are in a new section of the book, marked out by the expression *These are the generations*, which Genesis will use several times to introduce the next part of the account;[1] the whole focus of this part will be on events near and in *Eden*.

---

1.   See Genesis. 5:1, 6:9, 10:1, for instance.

As mentioned above, some scholars have suggested that Genesis 1:1–2:3 and the section starting in Genesis 2:4 are two separate accounts of creation, by different authors and from different time periods, pasted together (rather inelegantly) by a later editor; and that the second account cannot be harmonized with the first. It has also been pointed out that the general Hebrew word for God (*Elohim*) is used in Genesis 1, whereas in Genesis 2:4–3:24 he is called by his personal name (*Yahweh*) – this is taken as evidence that the accounts are from different sources.

On a more careful reading, however, the apparent difference shrinks. Much is due to the move from global to local perspectives. So, for instance, the statement that *no bush of the land had yet sprung up* does not mean there was no vegetation on Planet Earth (which would have contradicted 1:11-12), but that there was nothing growing in that particular place, prior to the coming of irrigation (the word translated *land* can refer to a local area, not necessarily the whole earth). Moreover, this second account, far from contradicting the first, presupposes it: how would 2:4 make sense without 1:1–2:3? We will also see, later in this chapter, that there is a very good and obvious reason why Genesis would now want to give a more personal name for God than it has done so far. Most significant, however, is the simple observation that there is an obviously logical sequence of thought between the great prologue of Genesis 1 and this new section, as we are introduced in turn to God, then us, then our relationship.[2]

Genesis 2:4-17, then, is not so much a separate creation account as a development from the first. There may be retrospective elements (for instance, we have already heard in 1:26-30 about the creation of humanity) but

2.   See also Matthew 19:4-5 for Jesus' view of the unity of Genesis 1 and 2.

essentially this new section moves the story on, taking us to the relationship between God and us. Carefully and emphatically, Genesis marshals three reasons why *no human will ever truly flourish except in friendship with the God of the Bible*.

We owe our whole existence to God (2:4-7)

Genesis 2:5 paints a strange picture of aridity in the land: nothing is growing. This is a dry place. And why? '... for the LORD God had not yet caused it to rain on the land, and there was no man to work the ground' (2:5). The point is that there is someone missing: man. We are in a Near Eastern semi-desert, which urgently needs human attention if it is to be cultivated. (It is possible that the slightly mysterious verse 6, whose first word can be translated *and*, describes some sort of irrigation, possibly an ancient Near-Eastern *qanat* system, which works from underground.) Genesis is re-emphasizing that the world needs the ruler God has appointed for it; creation is incomplete without him.

But there is not long to wait, for '... the LORD God formed the man of dust from the ground and breathed into his nostrils the breath of life, and the man became a living creature'(7). Man is here!

At this point, Genesis makes a point with a pun. The Hebrew word for *man* sounds very similar to the word for *ground.* Every atom, every molecule in us is derived only from the world about us; it just passes up the food chain.

I remember a TV ad for a well-known Irish butter. The campaign focused on the lushness of the grass that grows in Ireland. Presumably that is due to fertile soil and an ideal climate. Anyway, it makes its way into the cows, and then, of course, into the butter – which, as it then goes into us, presumably induces a feeling of well-being! We are what we eat; physically we are from the ground. True, we are made in the image of God; true, we are both the pinnacle and the heart of God's creative purposes. But, interestingly, God did not choose to make us of some indestructible, specially spiritual material, something different from the animals or the rest of creation. We are made of the same stuff: oxygen, hydrogen, carbon and the rest, bound into molecules of the same compounds that we walk across and breathe in every day.

This should humble us, and it certainly has a vulnerable feel to it. Indeed, we are not just from the ground, but of *dust from the ground*. Dust has a way of going back to being dust again. The Psalmist uses the same Hebrew word when he says of God that 'he remembers that we are but dust.'[3] We are not indestructible: if the man were to live for ever, he would have to have to eat from the tree of life (3:22). Our present bodies, says the Apostle Paul to the Corinthians, are of dust.[4]

And we ground-derived, made-of-the-dust people depend entirely on God for our existence. For as God made the first man, he *breathed into his nostrils the breath of life*. And so he does with us: as Paul told the Athenians, 'he gives to all mankind life and breath and everything.'[5] The ground, the dust and the breath all emphasise one thing: our total dependence on our Maker.

Have you ever paused to think just how dependent on things outside us God has made us to be? Our very design emphasizes to us again and again that we cannot survive as self-contained beings. We can survive only

---

3. Psalm 103:14

4. 1 Corinthians 15:42-49

5. Acts 17:25

weeks without food, days without water and minutes without air. We rely on the sun for all our energy; civilization quickly perishes without rain or rivers. We are the very opposite of being self-contained. Genesis 2 takes us back to our Creator and shows us that this is how our Creator has designed things to be. Ultimately, these are marks of our total dependence on him as the maker and giver of all that sustains us.

No wonder, then, that we are only going to flourish in relationship with God. We have not been designed to make it on our own. Genesis 2 is preparing us to see that the rebellion against the Creator described in chapter 3 is utter folly. We will see, when we get there, just how the relationship with the ground from which we have been made has been altered because we have declared independence.

There seems to be a widely held assumption that a person who is conscious that they depend on God must be, frankly, odd. The sane way through life is to keep well clear of all that. The 'religion' slots on the radio or TV must be at odd times of the day, very early or very late, with the main slots reserved for what really matters to sensible people. On the contrary, Genesis insists, the only sane way to live is in relationship with your Maker. To try to live in His world without Him is the odd choice.

This God's presence is where we will flourish (2:8-14)
Next, in Genesis 2:8, God takes the man and puts him in this garden he has made. It seems to have been a real place, for the rivers *Tigris* and *Euphrates* are mentioned, but the precise location remains uncertain. What is clear, however, is that it was gorgeous. 'And out of the ground the LORD God made to spring up every tree

that is pleasant to the sight and good for food' (9). There was plenty to drink, and the land was well-watered (10). Nearby there was *gold* (11, 12), and *bdellium* (12), which is a kind of perfume resin. There were treats for the eyes, the tongue, the tummy and the nose. No wonder the Hebrew word *Eden* is similar to the word for *delight*.[6] Imagine getting all this with the keys to your new home!

Indeed, God's sheer goodness and generosity are written all over his provision for the man. There is no holding back here! The details stress repeatedly the kindness and good intentions of the God who provides it all. Gold and sweet-smelling perfumes are not necessities but luxuries; we are not just in the supermarket but the duty-free shop! The Creator positively delights in providing an abundance for the man he has made.

And it is not just the goodness of God which is hinted at here, but the delight of this mysterious *garden*. There may be a particular significance in this, which would have been spotted by the first readers of Genesis. For some of the details of Eden – the gold, a tree, cherubim on guard (Gen. 3:24) and the smells – found echoes in the design and operation of the Tabernacle (and later the Temple), the place of meeting between God and his people.[7] It was like this in Eden, too; the place where God walked in the cool of the day (3:8). Here the man was in God's very presence, in close relationship with him. The Garden stands for that. And Genesis is telling us that that is a great place to be; it is the place of human flourishing.

---

6. Our word Paradise derives ultimately from the ancient Persian word for a walled garden.

7. See Exodus 29:42-46, 1 Kings 7:13-51.

This is enormously important, because there is a monster lie, which has done the rounds in everyone's life. We will encounter it in chapter 3, and it runs as follows: 'You will do badly in the presence of God. He is mean and a spoilsport; get close to him and your life will shrivel and be wasted. You will not flourish.' In 2008, an atheist group organised a poster campaign on London's buses. Their slogan was, 'There's probably no God, now stop worrying and enjoy your life.' The assumption was that if God is there at all, he's a killjoy. So we mustn't have anything to do with him if we want to enjoy life. Forget God; don't waste your life, go enjoy yourself.

But Genesis will not have us fall for this. God is good! His intentions are loving, and his provision ultra-generous. He is a great one to be with. Where are we to find real delight, real meaning, real fulfilment in life, other than in his presence? This, then, is Genesis' aim in telling us what a great place Eden was, and in emphasizing God's bumper kindness: that we might seek him, find him and discover his goodness for ourselves.

There is a powerful clue that this is Genesis' aim at this point. God is *named* in this chapter as the covenant God of Israel. It is striking that in chapter 1 he is simply called *God*, translating the Hebrew *Elohim*, but here in chapter 2 he is called *Yahweh Elohim*, using the name God gave Israel to call him.[8] This is represented in many English versions with capital letters, as *the LORD God*, which makes it look like just another title, but *Yahweh* is, in fact, God's personal name, distinguishing him from other deities known to ancient Israel (such as Baal or Molech). The difference between Genesis 1 and 2 is a bit like the difference between the

---

8.   Exodus 3:13-15

term 'The King' and 'King Charles': the latter tells us much more precisely who we're talking about. This sharpening of focus makes perfect sense at this point in Genesis, for the writer's very point is to show us *in whose company* we will flourish. That is why he now provides us with – so to speak – where to find him: this is the God of Israel, of the Bible. The emphasis could not be clearer. (This is the explanation of the difference between the names of God mentioned above: surveying the whole book, Jewish Hebrew scholar Umberto Cassuto noted that Genesis uses the word *Yahweh* of God particularly when speaking of relationship.[9])

In other words, we will not flourish simply by getting religious or vaguely thinking of any god, but only in relationship with *the* Lord of Israel, the God of the Bible – made known to us in Christ. He it is who made us; he it is whose nature is so generously to provide; he alone is the one in whom true delight is to be found. We need to know this, not only that we might find him, but that we might avoid the alternatives. For the lie that we will be worse off with God gains much of its energy from the sterility of other religions, and the disappointment that often follows.

So written all over this section is the goodness of the God of the Bible, and the delight which could be ours in his presence. With that comes the implied question: do you want this, if somehow it could be found? Surely this would be Paradise regained!

---

9.   See U. Cassuto, *A Commentary on the Book of Genesis*, Pt 1 (Jerusalem: Magnes, 1961), p. 87. As mentioned above, the view, still widespread in some critical commentaries, that Genesis 1 and 2 are from different sources, has as its centrepiece this apparent change in the name of God. The writer of Genesis 1:1–2:3 preferred Elohim and the writer of 2:4–4:26 preferred Yahweh Elohim, it is supposed. It does not seem to occur to these commentators that the same writer may have made this change in Genesis 2 precisely because he has a theological point to make. See Psalm 19 for another example of the same change made, when moving from the general to the particular.

God is the Ruler, so it is folly to rebel (2:15-17)

> The LORD God took the man and put him in the garden of Eden to work it and keep it. (2:15)

The Garden needed man to work it – to fulfil the responsibility given him in Genesis 1:26-28. As he is introduced to his beautiful surroundings, he is reminded again of God's marvellous provision: 'You may surely eat of every tree of the garden...'(16) . The emphasis again is on God's bountiful care: there is food everywhere, and plenty for the palate to savour.

Except for the fruit of one tree. '...but of the tree of the knowledge of good and evil you shall not eat, for in the day that you eat of it you shall surely die'(17). There is just this one prohibition. Don't eat from that one, or it will be the end of you. The rules of the Garden can hardly be described as onerous: in fact, there is only one! The rulebook would not have taken long to learn. The man has great freedom in filling his bowl with all sorts of different fruits; again, God is no spoilsport! But this one single rule is still there, and disaster will follow if it is broken.

Just what this mysterious *tree of the knowledge of good and evil* stands for, we will return to when we get to chapter 3, where there is more detail. All that matters at this point is that the tree is there, and that eating from the tree would be direct disobedience. We have seen already in the chapter that we have been made by God and depend on him, and that only in his presence will we truly flourish; now God warns that to rebel against him will bring disaster. We are reading, in fact, the very first covenant, or binding agreement, between God and man. The prohibited fruit and the warning that goes with it express the terms of the covenant: we can only flourish and enjoy a relationship with God if we are willing to submit to his rule, truly letting him be Lord of our lives.

How much we need to hear this! For if one lie is that the Lord of the Bible is mean, and that his presence is not a good place to be, a closely related one is that we will only really flourish as humans if we reject his rule over our lives, and decide to make our own way. We will see, from chapter 3 onwards, just how this attitude worked out, and what followed. God was not bluffing when he promised death to those who ate from the tree.

We see this lie worked out in every human heart; we also see specific examples worked out in society. In Western countries, the big con of the 1960s was the idea that we didn't need the God of the Bible's arrangements for marriage; it was time to move on from the old sexual mores and enjoy free love. Fun, fun, fun! Fifty years later, this gigantic experiment is generating results: heartache, shattered lives and the loneliest society on record. I cannot help writing this without thinking of the way that in 1978 Freddie Mercury sang *Don't stop me now, I'm having such a good time.* The song made it all sound good too. But in 1985, in an interview, he said: *You can have everything in the world and still be the loneliest man.* Six years later, he died a tragic death.

There are some lessons in history which, although repeated, never seem to get through. This is one. So Genesis wants us to know that we depend on the One who made us, and we will only flourish if we live in relationship with him, under his rule. His service is perfect freedom. Millions today continue to believe the con that we can do without him. Genesis is urging us not to make that mistake.

★ ★ ★

If you are a Christian today, what decisions do you face in which you are finding it hard to trust God, and what he says? Is there some course of action which you know from the Bible you should take, but are fearful of? Trust this God, for his purposes for you are entirely, totally good. His generosity is infinitely greater than we imagine.

If you are not yet a Christian, you may be wondering what you are letting yourself in for. Is trusting the God of the Bible going to ruin your life? This fear is there in many people's minds. Note well that as early as the second chapter of the Bible, God is addressing that fear. Part of the enjoyment of becoming a Christian is discovering for oneself, in personal experience, that the true and living God is indeed as generous and positive in his purposes for us as Genesis 2 says.

And there is more. Given God's generosity and determination to do the man good, it should not surprise us that, as we will see later, his dealings with us were not ended by our rebellion. Indeed, the Bible's story is one of persistent and astounding generosity on God's part. It should be no surprise that he was prepared to give a lot more so that once again we might enjoy this relationship with him. He gave no less than his one and only Son. And because of that, he promises all who will trust him a new heavens and a new earth that themselves resemble Eden – only bigger and better.[11]

We were made by God; we depend on him and will flourish only in relationship with him. Sixteen centuries ago, Augustine, the bishop of Hippo in North Africa, looked back on his conversion to Christ and wrote what must be his most famous prayer of praise, 'You have made us for yourself and our hearts are restless until they rest in you.'[12]

---

11. Compare the details in Revelation 21:1–22:6.

12. Augustine, *Confessions* (A.D. 397-8), translated by R. S. Pine-Coffin (Harmondsworth: Penguin Classics, 1961), I.I, p. 21.

EXTRA NOTE: WHAT KIND OF ACCOUNT IS GENESIS 2–3?

It is sometimes suggested that this account is purely a 'myth', and never intended to be read as actual history.[13] Could it be that it was never intended to describe things that really happened, but rather to be a timeless analysis of our human condition?

Most certainly, there are timeless principles here. When we read this story, we see ourselves. Genesis 2–3 makes sense of our world both in terms of what happened once, a long time ago, and what continues to happen; it is not just about the dawn of civilization but the world of the reader.

At the same time, the inclusion of geographical details, with four rivers named, including the *Tigris* and *Euphrates* (2:14), locates these events in a real place. We aren't in Narnia, but somewhere in Iraq or south-eastern Turkey (John Calvin, in his commentary on Genesis, even includes a map[14]). The formula, *These are the generations of* (2:4), is used later in Genesis to introduce narratives clearly intended to be understood as historical (5:1; 6:9; 10:1 and more). Moreover, the New Testament also reads Genesis 2–3 as telling us about real history. In Romans 5:12-21, the Apostle Paul talks about sin coming into the world, and it is clear that he regards Adam as a historical individual and the Fall as a historical event. It is clear from all of this that we cannot dismiss these chapters simply as a mirror held up to our world, without reference to a real, historical event: this is *not* just a 'timeless myth'.

We must also recognize that the account contains an unusual amount of symbolism in its details – items intended

---

13. I appreciate that the term 'myth' is itself very slippery. Time and again you will meet authors who deny that it necessarily means 'historically non-factual'. But the everyday use of the word certainly has that sense; moreover, whenever did you hear an account of something whose historicity is unchallenged being described as a myth?

14. John Calvin, *Commentaries on the first book of Moses called Genesis* (1563), Translated by John King (Grand Rapids: Baker, 1996), p. 120.

to speak of deeper realities. The Garden, as we have seen, seems to stand for the presence of God. Nakedness and fig leaves (2:25; 3:7) will express truth about relationships and what happens to them when we assert sinful autonomy. The Bible itself tells us that the serpent (3:1) is more than a reptile,[15] and, as we will see, there is more to the Tree of the Knowledge of Good and Evil than simply an attractive part of the orchard.[16] The use of symbolism in this account is much higher than in most Biblical narratives.

This might mean that the account is telling us real history, but in a 'non-literal' way – C. S. Lewis seems to have held to a version of this understanding of Genesis 2–3, as have others.[17] Seen this way, the account would resemble the prophet Nathan's retelling of King David's sin in 2 Samuel 12. But equally, the fact that something is symbolic does not rule it out, also, from having a real, physical existence – for instance, a flag is symbolic of a nation's power, but still a real piece of cloth, flying in the wind. To say something is 'symbolic' does not preclude its physical reality. Thus, the details here might be *both* symbolic *and* literal.

I dare venture no further! Either way, *what matters most is what these symbols point to.*

---

15. See Revelation 12:9; 20:2

16. Revelation 22:2

17. C. S. Lewis, *The Problem of Pain* (this edition, Glasgow: Collins, 1977), p. 59.

GENESIS 2:18-25

[18]Then the LORD God said, 'It is not good that the man should be alone; I will make him a helper fit for him.' [19]Now out of the ground the LORD God had formed every beast of the field and every bird of the heavens and brought them to the man to see what he would call them. And whatever the man called every living creature, that was its name. [20]The man gave names to all livestock and to the birds of the heavens and to every beast of the field. But for Adam there was not found a helper fit for him. [21]So the LORD God caused a deep sleep to fall upon the man, and while he slept took one of his ribs and closed up its place with flesh. [22]And the rib that the LORD God had taken from the man he made into a woman and brought her to the man. [23]Then the man said,

'This at last is bone of my bones
    and flesh of my flesh;
she shall be called Woman,
    because she was taken out of Man.'

[24]Therefore a man shall leave his father and his mother and hold fast to his wife, and they shall become one flesh. [25]And the man and his wife were both naked and were not ashamed.

9 Sex in Paradise
Genesis 2:18-25

Sex in Paradise – it sounds nice, doesn't it? And yet it also seems out of reach.

Genesis is moving in a carefully ordered sequence through the great essentials of our existence: God, humanity, and then the relationship between God and humanity. In Genesis 2:18-25, the focus is a relationship between people. It makes total sense as the next point in the flow of the account.

The particular relationship described at this point is the one that all our lives depend on: that between man and woman. Genesis now describes and celebrates that, and the picture it paints is deeply attractive. The LORD God sees the man, alone in the Garden, and from his side makes woman. The man is thrilled, and the chapter ends on a note of intimacy and openness between the pair of them.

Which of us does not want real, deep happiness in this area? The trouble is that the reality of our experience is often so very different. Love, delight and openness are what we long for, and we may experience much of this; but many people's stories are also of heartache, guilt, secrecy, loneliness, confusion and even hatred. And that can make it hard for us to listen to Genesis 2. What does it have to say to us, in the messy realities of our existence?

The New Testament answer is: a great deal. The great importance of this account is that here, in the Garden, we are in the world before the corrupting effect of sin, where 'what is' is the same as 'what ought to be'. If our lives now are like the bits of a jig-saw puzzle scattered on the table, Genesis 2 shows us the picture on the box. Comparing the picture with the scattered bits – the contrast with our present lives – will show us, with tragic clarity, just how devastating the effects of sin are. But the picture on the box is also a beautiful and practical blueprint for living. For the New Testament tells us how Jesus Christ has come to bring us back to God; and, having brought us back to God, he restores and repairs the lives of all who trust in him. He does this by making us back into the people we were made to be; he brings us back to the Paradise way.[1] This is why the New Testament takes these verses as the foundation for all its teaching on marriage and sex. In a world where there is so much confusion in this area, the value of this 'picture on the box' is incalculable.

So what does the paradise pattern look like?

The LORD God's provision (2:18-23)
Stamped all over this account, just as in the account of the Garden, is the continuing theme (from earlier in Genesis 2) of the LORD God's provision. When, as

---

1. See, for instance, Matthew 19:1-9.

a minister taking a wedding, I read out a sentence saying that 'marriage is a gift of God in creation', I am just teaching this passage.

The story begins with a lack. Everything in the Garden is so good, but for one thing: the man is alone. We are at a new phase in the story, echoing perhaps the way things were incomplete in 2:5-6, where the land needed man to work it. Now the man is here, but he needs 'a helper fit for him' (2:18). God brings the animals to the man, to see what he will call them, and the man names them, expressing his rule over them by giving them their names. 'Goat... dog... sheep...', says the man (though not in English, I think), but none is suitable for the role of *helper fit for him* that God knows the man needs. Yes, there is a relationship between the man and the animals, expressed by this naming. But they are not the answer.

I love our dog Rosie; all the family do. She is friendly to *nearly* all visitors to our house. But – whatever is said – a dog cannot be my best friend. Nor so for the first man: he needs another human being, his equal.

So the LORD God puts the man under what we might call the original general anaesthetic, and performs divine surgery. When the patient comes round, look who's here! She is not something different from him, as the animals are, but made from him, and of him. She is just right. So he bursts into a song, whose lyrics can be translated literally as: 'This one – at last! Bone of my bones, and flesh of my flesh. I shall call this one Woman for from man she was taken, this one!'[2] She's the one! She is like him, as the name he gives her suggests (for the Hebrew for woman,

---

2. Christopher Ash, *Marriage* (IVP, 2003) p. 121.

ishshah, is similar to the Hebrew for man, *ish*), yet she is not the same; she is woman, not man.

At this point, Genesis draws a lesson for us, in the present tense:

> Therefore a man shall leave his father and his mother and hold fast to his wife, and they shall become one flesh. (2:24)

As we will see, this chain of leaving-and-joining-and-one-flesh is a neat definition of marriage.

The whole emphasis, then, is on the LORD God's generous provision, in keeping with all his goodness already demonstrated in the Garden, with all its fruit and gold and rivers and perfumes. Here is a need beautifully, wonderfully met. Genesis is very, very positive about marriage. It is a good thing. It is emphatically not a necessary evil, or a way of life suitable only for the less religious (and not the clergy). No; it is, as the Anglican Prayer Book says, 'an honourable estate, instituted in the time of man's innocency'.[3]

The Shakers were a religious sect in eighteenth and nineteenth-century America, best known today for the elegant simplicity of their furniture. But they had one very peculiar practice: abstinence from sex. That, in the Shaker world, was how to be really religious. At their height in the mid-nineteenth century, they had 6,000 members; but by the early twenty-first century their numbers were down to half a dozen. Can you work out why?

We may need to relearn this lesson from Genesis in contemporary Western society. We certainly aren't

---

3. *The Book of Common Prayer* (1662), 'The form of solemnization of matrimony.'

negative about sex, but many are nervous about marriage. It may be we have seen too many marriages go wrong, and we are scared of the commitment. Of course, some would long to be married but, for one reason or another, have to wait, and this can be a painful struggle. Others, for very good reasons, wish to remain single.[4] But others hang back out of misplaced nerves. Marriage works; it is a great thing! If you are already married, thank God for his provision for you. You and your spouse are, as Jesus put it, 'what... God has joined together'.[5]

The LORD God's provision – for the world

Not only is marriage God's provision for us, but it is also part of his provision for the world. Christopher Ash, in his book *Marriage*,[6] has helpfully drawn attention to the fact that Genesis 2:18 follows Genesis 1:28:

> Be fruitful and multiply and fill the earth and subdue it and have dominion over the fish of the sea and over the birds of the heavens and over every living thing that moves on the earth.

Why isn't the man to be alone? Because his God-given task was to look after the Garden and rule the world. That was where he needed help: in serving God by fulfilling his God-appointed role. The man and woman can work together, and also reproduce; in this way, the planet is peopled and we can fulfil the responsibility God has given us. Marriage is, to quote the thought-provoking subtitle of Ash's book, *Sex in the service of God*.

---

4. See Paul's discussion of this in 1 Corinthians 7.

5. Matthew 19:6

6. Christopher Ash, *Marriage*.

This means that a couple who take Genesis 1 and 2 seriously as the foundation truth for their marriage will be outward-facing. They will spend time together, but also have an open home; they will pray together for others; they will seek between them to raise children who will be useful for God; they will spur each other on in their service of him.

We have a number of older married friends who remind me of this. Their affection for each other is obvious and delightful; but the warmth of their marriages spills over into an obvious love for those who know them and visit their homes. I remember when Rachel and I visited the minister who was to take our wedding and his wife, meeting up with them for marriage preparation. We came away from seeing them feeling twice as much in love! Their marriage is focused on loving and serving God and others – just as Genesis says it should be. If you're married, don't you want to be like that?

If you are not married, it is good to be reminded of this – that what matters most is our serving God in this world. Marriage is a wonderful provision of God which helps many people do this, but is not, in itself, the be-all-and-end-all of everything. Both marriage and singleness are spheres in which we can serve him, argues Paul in 1 Corinthians 7.

The LORD God's sequence: leaving then cleaving (2:24)

In verse 24, Genesis takes the pattern of this first marriage and applies it to us: this is how it will be.

> Therefore a man shall leave his father and his mother and hold fast to his wife, and they shall become one flesh.

This summary verse is seen as very important in the New Testament, where it is quoted four times. Perhaps more than any other verse in the Bible, it helps us understand what marriage actually is. It gives us the components of marriage, and it does so in a deliberate sequence.

First, *a man shall leave his father and mother*. Marriage means a change of relationship with one's family. The man leaves his father and mother (and so does his bride). In Western church weddings, this is symbolised by the bride walking up the aisle of the church with her father, her hand being given to the groom, and then her return down the aisle with her husband. In law, next-of-kin have been her parents (if they are alive); now, it is the spouse. A new relationship of great closeness is formed: the two *become one flesh*, with a loyalty which now supplants even that wonderfully close relationship of parents and child.

We need to heed this. In many families, the umbilical cord is very strong indeed. This is no bad thing, but it must not be allowed to strangle the marriage. In the U.K., mother-in-law jokes are a popular genre ('What's the definition of mixed feelings? Watching your mother-in-law drive your new car off a cliff!', etc.). While some of these jokes are a little unkind, the reality in many people's lives is that there is some fire behind the smoke, with parents who aren't really ready to let go and recognize the formation of a new relationship. If you are married, remember this, and if you have children who are getting married, remember it even more!

This truth also helps explain the difference between marriage and just moving in with your lover. In a relationship as powerful and intimate as that between man and woman, others are also involved – parents, and, by extension, society as a whole. In our privatized, me-only world view, we tend to think that all that matters are two consenting adults. But these wider relationships matter, too. Marriage is a device common to all societies that gives this relationship the public recognition that it needs because others are involved. It is this public recognition, stemming from here in Genesis, that is the all-important difference between marriage and cohabitation.

Secondly, the man shall *hold fast to his wife*. 'Holding fast' implies a very strong grip. In the famous language of the Authorised Version of the Bible, the word is *cleave*. In marriage, man and woman are bonded tightly. Remember that day at school when Smith played a nasty trick by bonding Teacher's trousers to Teacher's chair by leaving that blob of superglue?

Jesus picks this up when answering questions about divorce. He quotes this verse, attributing its authorship to God himself, and draws the lesson that the Creator's intention is that marriage be permanent. His point is: 'Therefore, what God has joined together, let not man separate.'[7] That is why divorce, rather like tearing apart two bits of paper which have been glued, is so terribly damaging. It is why, when we get married, we are right to make those awesome promises of permanence: 'For better, for worse, for richer, for poorer, in sickness and in health...till death us do part, and this is my solemn vow.'[8] Stick at it!

And then *they shall become one flesh*. Here is the closest of all human relationships, marked, maintained and matured by sex. And notice *where it comes in the sequence:* after the leaving and the cleaving. Right from the start, God's plan for sex is in the context of marriage. For

---

7.   Matthew 19:3-6

8.   Marriage service, Church of England.

it is his design that to enjoy something so intimate with another, we should love them enough to be fully committed to them, so that they are truly our 'other half'. The right place for the fire is the fireplace; if it gets round the rest of the house, it is a disaster. God's place for this great gift is the truly loving commitment in which each says, 'I intend to spend the rest of my life with you.' It stems, of course, from the fact that the God of the Bible specializes in faithfulness; it's integral to his own character, and it's something he prizes in us.

Keeping to this sequence sounds tough! We find it hard to trust; we think of a thousand reasons for breaking the sequence, including 'trying it out, to see if we are compatible' (even though the stats show that those who haven't slept together before marriage are *less* likely to split up). Or we reduce sex to a merely recreational activity. But might it just possibly be that the Maker's own instructions hold the key to real happiness? Our very surprise at them shows us just how much we need them.

The LORD God's pattern: male and female (2:22-25)
God's provision for the man is woman. It may seem obvious, but we need to see how strongly Genesis emphasizes this:

- verse 22: *and the rib... he made into a **woman** and brought her to the **man**.*

- verse 23: *... she shall be called **Woman**, because she was taken out of **Man**.*

- verse 24: *Therefore a **man** shall leave his father and his mother and hold fast to his **wife**...*

- verse 25: *And the **man** and his **wife** were both naked...*

In fact, the man-woman emphasis is even stronger than this suggests, for the word translated *wife* in verses 24 and 25 is the same word as *woman* in 22-23. 'Woman-man... woman-man... man-woman... man-woman' is how it runs.

This is God's creation pattern for marriage, and therefore for sex. So when, many centuries after the writing of Genesis, and in a completely different culture, the Apostle Paul sits at his desk in the Greek city of Corinth and writes his letter to the Christians at Rome, he still sees this as God's pattern and plan, for in Genesis 2, 'what is' is 'what ought to be'. This is why he describes homosexual relations as *contrary to nature* and says that those who engaged in them gave up natural relations.[9] Commenting on these verses in Romans, Professor Charles Cranfield writes:

> By 'natural' and 'contrary to nature' Paul clearly means 'in accordance with the Creator's intention' and 'contrary to the Creator's intention' respectively. It is not impossible that Paul had some awareness of the great importance which 'nature' had in Greek thought for centuries; that he was aware of its use in contemporary popular philosophy is very likely. But the decisive factor in his use of it is his biblical doctrine of creation.[10]

In Genesis 2, then, marriage (and therefore sex) is between a man and a woman. Much teaching in the rest of the Bible applies this.[11]

This is a hard thing to say in our social and political climate; the bits of the jigsaw are well and truly scattered!

---

9.   Romans 1:26, 27

10. C. E. B. Cranfield, *Romans: A Shorter Commentary* (Edinburgh: T. and T. Clark, 1985), p. 35.

11. e.g. 1 Corinthians 6:9-11; 1 Timothy 1:10

But how urgently, and with all compassion, we need to be honest about what the Bible says.[12] We will not help anyone – least of all those struggling with same-sex attraction – by failing to be clear about our Maker's loving purposes.

The LORD God's ordering (2:18-23)

There is also an ordering of the relationship between the man and the woman. He is put there to look after the world; she is described as his *helper*. He names her (2:23), not the other way round. It is to him, in the first instance, that responsibility is given for keeping the command in 2:16. And there is a sequence: he is made first, she comes second.

These might not strike us as significant notes in the text (although at the term *helper* there is already a hint), were it not for the fact that the New Testament picks this up as the basis of its teaching that in marriage and family, the ultimate responsibility rests with the husband; and that, in the local church, taking its model from the family, overall leadership responsibility must also rest with a man. This very passage in Genesis 2 – and particularly the sequence of creation – is referred to by Paul in both 1 Corinthians 11:8-9 and 1 Timothy 2:11-15, but it would not be exaggerating to suggest that all the New Testament teaching about male headship in marriage (such as in Ephesians 5) and church assumes its viewpoint.

Is Paul making a Corinthian mountain out of a Genesis molehill by reasoning from the fact that the man came first? I don't think so. We will see, when we get

---

12. It is to be welcomed that many churches are now taking more seriously proper pastoral support for those who struggle with unwanted same-sex attraction. See also Sam Allberry, *Is God Anti-Gay?* (London: The Good Book Company, 2013).

to Genesis 3, that Genesis sets great store by sequence. Moreover, in 3:17 God holds the man ultimately responsible for what happened. The Apostles were not inventing something new, but picking up the clues Genesis lays. And note that this pattern is here in this passage, before we get to the fall of humanity; it is there as the Creator's ideal, not simply the outcome of human sin. (If, at this point, you are finding this difficult to bear, please see the extra note at the end of this chapter, on 'chauvinism'.)

Since the Genesis pattern is God's creation order, it is no surprise that the New Testament sees this as a pattern for those who, in Christ, are part of God's new creation order. It should be reflected in the life of a church family, and in the lives of each married couple. Churches should seek to see this pattern honoured in their common life. Wives should think through what it means to be helpers of their husbands. And husbands need to take responsibility. How many wives would love to see their husbands taking more of a lead (including in the spiritual life of the home)! As we will see in Genesis 3, Adam was the first of a long line of men who have abdicated theirs.

Everything in the Garden was... (2:25)

> And the man and his wife were both naked and were not ashamed. (25)

What is this – an ad for nudism? No; it's a beautiful picture of something which matches our deepest longings: real intimacy with each other. Here is an openness in relationship, a nothing-to-hide pleasure in one another's company. This is God's breathtaking plan for marriage.

But we cannot read this section without ending where we began, recognizing that humanity's experience of marriage and sex is so far from this! We might crave this kind of openness and intimacy, but too often it seems beyond us. Sin's dreadful effects are nowhere seen more clearly than in its spoiling of this relationship, scattering the jigsaw pieces. You personally may have felt some of the pain of that, just reading through this chapter.

So where did it all go wrong?

EXTRA NOTE: GENESIS AND MALE CHAUVINISM

We have seen that Genesis 2 is the foundation for the rest of the Bible's teaching on male responsibility and headship. Many today find this ordering very problematic, and for good reason. For, once again, we are surveying the scattered bits of the jig-saw. In particular, we live in a world where we experience, again and again, the ugliness of male mistreatment of women. It is moving to read of the heroism of the Suffragettes in early twentieth-century England, some of whom grew up in families where the women were abused. We look around our world and see the dreadful subjugation of women in some religions. We think of the damage that could be done to a sense of self-worth by any suggestion that a woman is somehow inferior. Does Genesis open the door to an ugly chauvinism?

Not at all. We need to see what the text is *not* saying. Most emphatically, it is not saying that women are worth less than men. The term *helper* is, in fact, used in the Old Testament a number of times to refer to God himself, the *helper* of Israel.[13] Because we live in a society which measures someone's worth by their power, we automatically assume

---

13. For instance, Psalms 10:14; 118:7.

that when one helps another, the helper is worth less than the one helped. Christians, of course, should know better, because our Lord Jesus himself served his Father, but is equally God; indeed he came to serve us, who are not God! The difference in Genesis between men and women is emphatically one of *role*, not *worth*.

Nor does Genesis imply that (as in some cultures) the men can laze about while their women do all the menial chores. Nor does it suggest for a moment that men can ignore their families. Rather, what Genesis 2 does give us is God's beautiful creation design; an order that cuts a radical path between chauvinism, on the one hand, and the foolish pretence that there is no difference, on the other. God gives man, it seems, the final responsibility in the relationship. And this is before sin, before the disruption of the Fall; it is God's creation order.

Having seen what Genesis 2 does not say, we also need Genesis' help to understand why this is such a painful and emotive issue for us (indeed, your blood may be at a higher-than-usual pressure just reading this!). The answer comes in Genesis 3. When we get to Genesis 3:16, we will see that one result of human sin is the spoiling of the relationship between the man and the woman. We will explain this when we reach it; but at the moment we should note that the picture of happy headship is replaced by one of chauvinism, exploitation, subjugation and competition. And our problem is that this sort of behaviour is so much part of our experience that when we read Genesis 2, or the New Testament teaching on headship, we can jump to the conclusion that any sense of husbandly headship and responsibility must be wrong.

Think of it like one of those distorting mirrors, of the kind you get at amusement arcades or even with the software on computer webcam. A handsome face can be stretched and squeezed to look ugly and frightening. Just so, sin distorts a beautiful picture. Genesis 2 shows us what that beautiful picture originally looked like, and Genesis 3 shows us the distortions. *Do not be put off the original by the distortions.* God's purpose for his redeemed people is to return to that original, not to avoid it.[14]

---

14. I have located one possible source of this confusion. In the generally very helpful 'Index of allusions and verbal parallels' at the end of the UBS Greek New Testament – the standard version used by many ministers, academics and theological students – Paul's teaching on headship in 1 Corinthians 11:3 and 14:34, Ephesians 5:22 and Colossians 3:18, is linked to Genesis 3:16 and not, as it should be, to Genesis 2:20-21.

GENESIS 3:1-6

[1]Now the serpent was more crafty than any other beast of the field that the LORD God had made.

He said to the woman, 'Did God actually say, "You shall not eat of any tree in the garden"?' [2]And the woman said to the serpent, 'We may eat of the fruit of the trees in the garden, [3]but God said, "You shall not eat of the fruit of the tree that is in the midst of the garden, neither shall you touch it, lest you die."' [4]But the serpent said to the woman, 'You will not surely die. [5]For God knows that when you eat of it your eyes will be opened, and you will be like God, knowing good and evil.' [6]So when the woman saw that the tree was good for food, and that it was a delight to the eyes, and that the tree was to be desired to make one wise, she took of its fruit and ate, and she also gave some to her husband who was with her, and he ate.

10 So what went wrong?

Genesis 3:1-6

What has gone wrong with the world? Genesis 3 is the foundation of the Bible's answer, and as such is one of the most important chapters in all of Scripture. In Genesis 1–2, everything has been good; but by Genesis 4, we have reached the world we are familiar with: one of murder, heartache and alienation from God. How did we get from one to the other? With great economy of style, the chapter in between takes us to the very heart of the human problem. Every line is packed with meaning and significance.

The fact that the account involves a talking serpent, nude people, some fruit and various fig leaves has given fruitful (if you'll excuse the expression) material to many artists. Indeed, it is hard to read this pasage without thinking of an unreal-looking, scantily clad Adam and Eve, with just enough long hair and fig leaves to cover the essentials, grabbing some rosy-coloured fruit. And we find ourselves asking: what was going on? Was it all to do with sex? Was that the forbidden fruit, or was it something else which was naughty but nice? What's the harm in eating a piece of fruit, anyway?

We need to hurry from our preconceived ideas to the text itself. For what Genesis teaches here has, in fact, enormous power to explain our world. Each moment in the story is loaded with meaning.

The serpent and his strategy (3:1-4)

In verse 1, we are introduced to a new character:

> Now the serpent was more crafty than any other beast of the field that the LORD God had made. He said....

Two questions arise: how a serpent could possibly talk? And how, in God's good world, there could possibly exist a creature made by God which is opposed to him? The truth is that the text answers neither question. As with the rest of the Bible, we are told only what we need to know, not everything we would like to know. It does seem significant that the serpent is a *beast of the field*, for what is about to take place will involve a reversal of the creation order. The man and woman have been given dominion over the animals (1:26-28), but here they are about to capitulate to one of them: they will not be able to wriggle out of their responsibility by claiming that they were overwhelmed by a superior force. Readers of the New Testament will also know that the serpent is identified there with the devil.[1] But we are getting ahead of ourselves.

There is, however, a vital question which Genesis does address: how does the serpent get his way, and entice the woman and man to do exactly what God has commanded them not to do? In Genesis 2:16-17, there was a clear prohibition:

---

1.   Revelation 12:9; 20:2

> And the LORD God commanded the man, saying,
> 'You may surely eat of every tree of the garden, but of
> the tree of the knowledge of good and evil you shall not
> eat, for in the day that you eat of it, you shall surely die.'

But that is exactly the command the man and woman
now break. Amazingly, he never actually says, 'Go on –
eat the fruit,' yet he is entirely successful. How?

The answer Genesis gives is that he uses a series of
top-quality lies. Like the very best falsehoods, they sound
similar to the truth; that is how they find a hearing. In
particular, they are lies about God and his nature.

He starts by encouraging Eve to **doubt God's goodness.**

> Did God actually say, 'You shall not eat of any tree in
> the garden?'(1b).

The serpent's implication, of course, is that God is
restrictive and harsh. He had put the man and woman in
that beautiful garden, yet *all* the trees had a 'Don't eat the
fruit' label on them. It seems so very mean. And what is
clever about this suggestion is that it *sounds* so similar to
God's original command (2:16-17), even though it is in
fact quite different.

Eve seems to spot this in her reply:

> We may eat of the fruit of the trees in the garden, but
> God said, 'You shall not eat of the fruit of the tree that
> is in the midst of the garden, neither shall you touch it,
> lest you die.'(2-3)

Far from being restrictive, God is happy for them to
eat anything they like: the prohibition extends to one
tree only. But there is a clue that the serpent has gained

a foothold in her mind: even in her generally accurate reply, she says that God has banned *touching* the tree of the knowledge of good and evil. Strictly speaking, he had not; she has added to the Word of God. Is this just a hint that she is beginning to believe part of the serpent's lie?

The serpent is not long in replying, and this time his challenge is more direct. He makes her **doubt God's judgment**:

'You will not surely die...' (4b)

We could put the serpent's words like this: 'God is bluffing when he threatens dire consequences in eating this fruit. There will, in fact, be no death, no evil consequences. For the truth is that eating from the tree will actually bring benefits, which God wants (as the spoilsport he is) to keep for himself! 'For God knows that when you eat of it your eyes will be opened, and you will be like God, knowing good and evil' (3:5). This is why he threatens death – he doesn't want you to have all this extra knowledge. But, let me tell you, God's threat is entirely idle.'

This is worth pausing on. For although, at one level, Genesis is recounting a unique historical event, if it is true that the serpent is in some way to be identified with the devil, his tactics are surely worth noting. Could it be that he does some of his work today in similar ways? The Apostle Paul thought so, as he told the Christians in Corinth: 'I am afraid that as the serpent deceived Eve by his cunning, your thoughts will be led astray from a sincere and pure devotion to Christ.'[2] What is the cause of his concern? 'False apostles, deceitful workmen, disguising

2.   2 Corinthians 11:3

themselves as apostles of Christ. And no wonder, for even Satan disguises himself as an angel of light.'[3] Could it be, then, that the devil still uses the same old tricks?

For instance, we are often conned into doubting that **God has our best interests at heart**. God is against sex, we are told (even though it is his invention). He is against pleasure, or material goods (even though he has made a material world). We will be the losers if we follow him (even though he is our Maker, who is better placed than anyone to make us flourish). From time to time I meet people who are not Christians and who think the cost of turning to God will be too much for them. Even amongst Christians the lie lurks, welling up as a fear that following him wholeheartedly (perhaps in this or that step of discipleship) cannot result in our good.

We have already seen how strongly Genesis 2 rebuts that lie, by speaking of God's lavish generosity. I presume it needs to shout this loudly because we are naturally unwilling to believe its straightforward logic. God desires our happiness, and he is to be enjoyed! Yet the serpent's lie about God's goodness continues to slither under the door of our thinking in all sorts of areas. The challenge it carries is for each of us actively to trust that the living God has our highest interests, our personal flourishing, on his heart. How many temptations to evil gain their energy from not believing this! If we think God's way is not for our best, we will soon find a way of our own. Here, for instance, is the person who has left their spouse and is seeing someone else; when challenged that they must repent, they believe that if they did so, their world would fall apart. Or here is the person who has heard about Christianity, and is beginning to suspect that it is true, but

---

3.   2 Corinthians 11:13-14

is reluctant to take things further for fear that they will lose out. Both have believed versions of the serpent's lie: that God does not have their best interests at heart.

There is also the serpent's lie about **God's judgment**. This has a natural appeal to us, for we would all love to believe that actions don't have consequences. The man who spends Saturday night getting drunk would love to live in a world where his head didn't hurt on Sunday morning, and the profligate spender would rather live in a world where debts are not collected. And we take this desire further, and tell ourselves that there is no divine judgment, and no ultimate accountability. 'My God would not send anyone to hell!', we say, despite the fact that the world is so obviously crying out for justice.

Or the lie can be perpetuated more subtly. At the crematorium, the family hear the minister take Uncle Jack's funeral. They know he was a rogue, but the minister puts together a selection of hymns and Scripture readings which assure everyone that Uncle Jack is now in a better place. He probably isn't, but we want to think he is (and thank the vicar!), because if Jack can make it, so can we. The casualty, of course, is Christian commitment. Deep down, a god who doesn't care about how Uncle Jack lived allows us to carry on as we are – for *we* don't need to bother either. And he isn't a god worth bothering with, is he? It all suits us very well.

We should take careful note that in both the case of God's goodness and God's judgment, *the serpent's tactic is to create a false impression of God himself.* So much temptation gains its energy from lies and misunderstandings about God! For instance, much of the present moral confusion dividing the older denominations of the churches in the Western world has, at its source, theological confusion:

prod someone who wants to rewrite Christian ethics, and you may well find that they have already rewritten their understanding of God. Genesis teaches us that *temptation can work by means of lies distorting the truth about God, which thus make sin seem sensible and attractive.* How urgent and important it is, then, that we are clear about what he is really like, and are not taken in by the serpent's lies.

The heart of the matter: wanting to be like God, knowing good and evil (3:5)

What does the serpent mean when he says of the tree that '...when you eat of it your eyes will be opened, and you will be like God, knowing good and evil' (5)? What sort of extra knowledge is promised when their eyes will be opened? It cannot simply be the knowledge of right and wrong, as if, in their innocence, Adam and Eve did not know the difference. We have already seen that, quite clearly, Eve knew that God had prohibited eating from the tree. Instead, we must ask in what sense *God* knows good and evil. He cannot know it exactly as we do, as a set of principles over and above himself that he has discovered, for there is nothing over him. Good and evil are good and evil only because he decrees them so, as expressions of his own character and wisdom. Therefore, *his* knowledge of good and evil is the knowledge of one who *decides* on these categories.[4] A similar expression is used elsewhere in the Old Testament of the law-making role of the king, for instance when King Solomon prays 'Give your servant therefore an understanding mind to govern your people, that I may discern between good and evil...'[5]

---

4. For expansion of this point, see the commentaries by Blocher, Calvin and Wenham.

5. 1 Kings 3:9

The serpent's appeal to our first parents, then, was to acquire the same wisdom as God; in other words, to take upon themselves those decisions which are rightly his. They were being tempted to make up the rules for themselves. This is the significance, at the deepest level, of the taking of the fruit from the tree of the knowledge of good and evil. It isn't just law-breaking; it is law-making. It is making up my own personal moral code; it is doing things my way; it is an expression of autonomy. It is, by implication, a declaration of independence from the One who alone has the right to set the rules.

We could picture it this way. I hurtle down the road at 150 mph and am pulled over by the police for speeding. I insist that I have broken no rules, because at this time on a Wednesday there is no limit. 'Really?', says the officer, 'Where did you get that idea from?' 'Actually, *I* make up the rules round here,' I reply.

What a splendid scheme that is! If I make up the rules, I can make up rules that I keep. I can feel good about that; I can even pat myself on the back for being a fine, moral person. Of course, the real God is an inconvenience to me, but I can easily enough redesign him, working out my own version of religion. I talk of God and the things of God, but the real God in my life is myself. This is the knowledge the serpent offers with his appealing promise that *your eyes will be opened, and you will be like God.* But, of course, in the face of the real God, this is rebellion. The word is not too strong. It is at the heart of what the Bible will go on to call sin.

The deed is done (3:6)
It is all over in a flash.

> So when the woman saw that the tree was good for food, and that it was a delight to the eyes, and that the

tree was to be desired to make one wise, she took of its fruit and ate, and she also gave some to her husband who was with her, and he ate. (6)

The deed itself is so quick: she eats, she gives, he eats. And why not? There are three good reasons for doing so, itemized like bullet points: GOOD FOR FOOD, DELIGHT TO THE EYES, GOOD FOR WISDOM.

Notice how Genesis lets us into the woman and man's thinking. Eating the fruit is very appealing! Who would refuse? Certainly not Adam: he follows his wife's suggestion without hesitation. Yet at the same time, what a big thing this apparently small action is. Every part of the man and woman is involved: their appetites (*good for food*), their minds (*desirable for gaining wisdom*) and their wills (*they took*). And the prohibition they ignore is God's only one. They want to be *like God*, and with their whole personalities they break his whole law.

This, then, is the root of our human problem: rebellion against God. It is this which stands at the heart of the Bible's analysis of what's gone wrong. And we should be in no doubt that this is no minor peccadillo, but instead, enormously serious. For God alone has the right to be God.

At one end of the House of Lords in London stands a magnificent gilded throne, where the Queen sits when she delivers her annual speech to Parliament. One does not need to be an ardent royalist to think that for anyone else to sit on it on that great day would be unthinkable, or to wonder what on earth would happen when the Queen herself arrived. But in Genesis 3:6 humanity has taken its seat quite firmly in what is God's rightful place. What, then, will happen next? And what will be the longer-term consequences?

GENESIS 3:7-13

[7]Then the eyes of both were opened, and they knew that they were naked. And they sewed fig leaves together and made themselves loincloths.

[8]And they heard the sound of the LORD God walking in the garden in the cool of the day, and the man and his wife hid themselves from the presence of the LORD God among the trees of the garden. [9]But the LORD God called to the man and said to him, 'Where are you?' [10]And he said, 'I heard the sound of you in the garden, and I was afraid, because I was naked, and I hid myself.' [11]He said, 'Who told you that you were naked? Have you eaten of the tree of which I commanded you not to eat?' [12]The man said, 'The woman whom you gave to be with me, she gave me fruit of the tree, and I ate.' [13]Then the LORD God said to the woman, 'What is this that you have done?' The woman said, 'The serpent deceived me, and I ate.'

11 Edengate
Genesis 3:7-13

It's become part of our language. Ever since the Watergate burglary in 1972 and the subsequent cover-up, the word-ending *-gate* has been applied to episodes in public life where there is a deliberate attempt to conceal some wrongdoing. Let me now add to the list: *Edengate.* We are in the Garden of Eden, and the man and woman have just eaten the very fruit God has commanded them not to eat. They have wanted to be like him, knowing good and evil. Just as in the original Watergate scandal, when an apparently small act had momentous consequences, so it is here. From now on, Genesis 3 will recount for us the disaster that follows.

Cover-up (3:7)
The first casualty of the rebellion is openness. Genesis 3:7:

> Then the eyes of both were opened, and they knew that they were naked. And they sewed fig leaves together and made themselves loincloths.

The cover-up begins! They wanted wisdom, and all that happened was that they realized that they were naked. But this is no longer the nakedness without shame that they have enjoyed (2:25); now they need to cover things up. We could, to take a cue from the cover-up of the Watergate burglary in 1972, call this Edengate!

The cover-up is surely inevitable: once we start to live life according to our own desires, we can no longer trust each other. There will be things in our lives which we don't want each other to know about. We don't quite trust one another, because we don't know what each would do if they knew all about us.

The fig leaves in our lives take all sorts of forms. We pretend to be what we are not; we are one thing to one person, another to another. We spin the truth to make it presentable. We lock away our secrets; we clear the history on our web browsers; we stick stuff in the shredder; we are less than candid at a thousand points; we dread embarrassment. We are private, and need to be private, for we have stuff to blush about.

In 2009, the UK Parliament was rocked by a scandal over expenses. It turned out that some Members of Parliament had been claiming from public funds for what most of us would call personal luxuries. There was a public outcry as more and more details emerged of what had been going on. The reputation of a great national institution was crumbling. Eventually, the Parliamentary authorities realized that the only way to rescue the situation was to demonstrate some openness, so that trust could be restored. So they took the initiative and published the details of every Member's expenses on the official website. But when this went live, the web pages were covered by huge black patches, with the most sensitive details still covered up! The truth was simply too embarrassing to tell.

The tragedy is that we all crave, deep down, an intimacy and trust that allows us to be real with each other. There is a part of us that longs to be open, and to find the kind of friendship in which we really can be accepted as we are. But, with sin in the world, that has become an elusive goal.

Hide and seek (3:8-10)

What happens next makes clear that the man and woman are not just hiding from each other, but from God himself.

> And they heard the sound of the LORD God walking in the garden in the cool of the day, and the man and his wife hid themselves from the presence of the LORD God among the trees of the garden. (8)

There is a friendly intimacy in the picture of the LORD walking in their garden, sharing it with them; but now, like naughty children whose parents have found what they are up to, they hide. Did you ever do that? It is utterly futile, yet it is the inevitable instinct of the guilty.

So the man and woman hide, as hide they must: if we've been trying to make up the rules for ourselves, we aren't going to like it when the real God comes along. He calls out to the man and the woman, 'Where are you?' (9). The man replies with embarrassment (10); he has been found out. (They have not travelled far: they are still in the Garden, perhaps not realizing – as will become dreadfully clear later in Genesis 3 – that what they have actually done deserves banishment. We tend to underestimate the seriousness of sin.)

It is often suggested that we humans naturally seek God. There is a grain of truth here, for it is true that God 'has put eternity into man's heart,'[1] which means that we will never be fully satisfied until we have found our Maker. For this reason, we experience restlessness, and wonder why. But the picture in the Garden is not of people seeking God. Yes,

---

1. Ecclesiastes 3:11

there is a game of hide-and-seek going on, but *it is God who is doing the seeking, and the man and woman who are hiding.*

This is the very opposite of what we are often led to believe. God, if he is there at all, is assumed to be remote and elusive; our need is to search for him. This, it is suggested, is a difficult, uncertain process, with no sure outcome – as if it were in fact God hiding in the trees of the Garden, while we do the seeking! And yet Genesis says that the opposite is true. As John's Gospel tells us:

> And this is the judgment: the light has come into the world, and people loved the darkness rather than the light because their deeds were evil. For everyone who does wicked things hates the light and does not come to the light, lest his deeds should be exposed.[2]

At a week of special events in a university, I was talking to a student who told me that he liked to think of God as a mystery. 'Do you want him to *stay* a mystery?', I asked. 'Actually, I do', came the reply. It suited him to think of God as elusive, because then he could be elusive himself. This was my own position, until Christ got hold of me.

But the wonderful truth is that, though we are not seeking God, he is seeking us. Genesis 3:9 is a remarkable verse, for here, straight after humanity's wilful rebellion, *God is seeking them.* Of course, God has no need to ask the man his whereabouts, and he certainly has no obligation to bother, but he does. The very first question that God ever asks in the Bible is the same question a parent asks as it seeks a child that has run off. It is a question which will run from Genesis through the whole Bible story, as God sends into the world one who comes 'to seek and save the lost.'[3] He is still seeking us today. If you

---

2.   John 3:19-20

3.   Luke 19:10

are a Christian today, it is because God said, 'Where are you?' and came after you. Confidence that God does that should spur us to be persistent in making Christ known.

The blame game (3:11-13)

When the LORD God confronts the man with his actions, asking him what he has done (Gen. 3:11), the man's answer is a classic in passing the buck. Indeed, when reading verse 12 out loud, it is hard to know where to put the emphasis. Is it:

'The woman whom you gave to be with me, she gave me fruit of the tree, and I ate'?

Or is it:

'The woman whom you gave to be with me, she gave me fruit of the tree, and I ate'?

Is Adam blaming his wife, or God, who gave her to him? The answer is probably both; but in either case, Adam takes no personal responsibility.

Things are no better when God turns to the woman. '"What is this that you have done?" The woman said, "The serpent deceived me, and I ate."' As the old gag has it, Adam blamed Eve, Eve blamed the snake, and the snake didn't have a leg to stand on! What is missing is any sense of personal responsibility. All this is someone else's fault – either the other person's, or God's, for letting all this happen. Does that sound familiar? How often sin is not our fault:

'I was having a bad day!'
'It was my upbringing!'
'Have you any idea the *pressure* I was under?'
'It was my environment!'
'It was my wife!'
'My hormones made me do it!'
'Who is the fool who put that traffic light *there*?'

We are so used to it that we hardly notice. But, as we have seen already, it is a denial of our humanness, for God has given us the dignity of being responsible for our actions.

Notice another unpleasant development: fractures are now appearing between the man and his wife. Contrast the man's joy at her arrival in 2:23 ('This at last is bone of my bones and flesh of my flesh..') with the sheer resentfulness he shows here in 3:12 ('The woman whom you gave to be with me...'). The honeymoon is well and truly over. The rebellion was against God, but it has set the first couple at odds. Sin is like that: it not only offends God, but separates us from each other. When I want to be like God, making up the rules for myself, and you do the same, the place isn't big enough for the two of us. When I have things to hide, I will not let you right into my life. When we are found out, we will blame each other.

Did Adam and Eve think of any of this as they listened to the serpent's lies? He had promised so much! He insinuated that it was only because God was a spoilsport that he didn't want them to enjoy the goodies that would come from eating that fruit. But the reality is so very different. Already there is a bitter taste: shame, blame and mistrust. *All this – and we have not yet even got to God's judgment in the matter!* Sin is like that: it promises wonders, but delivers only heartache.

When, in the first half of Genesis 2, we are told in emphatic terms that we will only flourish in the presence of our Creator God, God is not bluffing. When we ask for whose sake God gives his law, the answer is that it is for ours. Ponder this section of Genesis, because the first lie in history – that God does not have our best interests at heart when he calls us to live under his rule – is still one of the most widely believed. The cold light of experience shows it to be a deadly deception.

GENESIS 3:14-24

¹⁴The LORD God said to the serpent,

'Because you have done this,
    cursed are you above all livestock
    and above all beasts of the field;
on your belly you shall go,
    and dust you shall eat
    all the days of your life.
¹⁵I will put enmity between you and the woman,
    and between your offspring and her offspring;
he shall bruise your head,
    and you shall bruise his heel.'

¹⁶To the woman he said,
'I will surely multiply your pain in childbearing;
    in pain you shall bring forth children.
Your desire shall be for your husband,
    and he shall rule over you.'

¹⁷And to Adam he said,
'Because you have listened to the voice of your wife
    and have eaten of the tree
of which I commanded you,
    "You shall not eat of it",
cursed is the ground because of you;
    in pain you shall eat of it all the days of your life;
¹⁸thorns and thistles it shall bring forth for you;
    and you shall eat the plants of the field.
¹⁹By the sweat of your face
    you shall eat bread,
till you return to the ground,
    for out of it you were taken;
for you are dust,
    and to dust you shall return.'

²⁰The man called his wife's name Eve, because she was the mother of all living. ²¹And the Lord God made for Adam and for his wife garments of skins and clothed them.

²²Then the Lord God said, 'Behold, the man has become like one of us in knowing good and evil. Now, lest he reach out his hand and take also of the tree of life and eat, and live for ever—' ²³therefore the Lord God sent him out from the garden of Eden to work the ground from which he was taken. ²⁴He drove out the man, and at the east of the garden of Eden he placed the cherubim and a flaming sword that turned every way to guard the way to the tree of life.

12 Mixed-up world
Genesis 3:14-24

In a world governed by a good and all-powerful God, why is our experience of life so mixed? There is so much to enjoy, but so much prevents our enjoyment of it. There is grandeur, beauty and pleasure, but also frustration, futility and suffering of many kinds. We live in a world of astonishing beauty but also agonizing pain.

The second half of Genesis 3 begins the Bible's explanation of this, as the LORD God announces how he will respond to the rebellion in the Garden. Genesis marks God's speech to the serpent, the woman and the man with great emphasis, moving from prose to verse, as if to make it stick in our minds. So it should: this passage has great power to explain our bafflingly mixed-up world.

What God says and does here may strike us, at first sight, as rather surprising, and we may find ourselves wondering why his sentence for the serpent, the man and the woman takes the form that it does. But we will see that there is a pattern to it. We will also see that this passage in Genesis has enormous power to make sense of our puzzlingly mixed experience of life. So much so, I venture, that we won't really understand our personal situations without it. For in these mixed experiences God has a message for us.

The curses (3:14-19)
God addresses all three players in the story with what have become known as the 'curses'. We instinctively find that difficult, because we associate curses with off-the-handle, bad-tempered language; but in God's case, this is his settled, controlled, holy and wise response to rebellion in the world he has made.

He starts with **the serpent** (3:14-15). Because of what he has done, he is 'cursed above all the livestock and above all the beasts of the field.' He is genuinely despicable, and will be reduced to a life of slithering in the dust. And, God says, 'I will put enmity between you and the woman, and between your offspring and her offspring.' At face value, this looks as if it is about venomous snakes, but this is not a Just So story about a particular kind of reptile; there is obviously more to it. *This* serpent, after all, is one who talks! As we have already noted, the New Testament understands the serpent of the Garden to represent the devil himself – another wily, camouflaged and lethal being. And the Bible shows examples of how, down through history, humanity has endured his attacks. He afflicts Job;[1] he cripples a woman for eighteen years;[2] he tempts Jesus in the desert;[3] he is even busy in the churches. We live

---

1. Job 2:7

2. Luke 13:16

3. Matthew 4:1-11

in a world where his enmity is to be expected, and the picture of a snake – slithering and vicious – illustrates this vividly.

But he is ultimately doomed, for the outcome of the conflict between the woman's offspring and the serpent is that 'he shall bruise your head, and you shall bruise his heel.' In a kind of poetic justice, having triumphed over humanity, he will be beaten by humanity. His defiance of the living God must, in the end, meet a horrible punishment – though not without a terrible struggle. Already, we find ourselves asking: when and how will this happen? (We will return to this shortly.)

Next, **the woman** (16). Her family life is to be spoilt. God says he will 'greatly increase her pain in childbearing.' No doubt in the first instance this refers to childbirth, but perhaps the second part of the phrase ('in pain you shall bring forth children') may hint that the whole process of having and bringing up children is in view. It is such a blessing – yet what heartaches can go with it! One of life's most sublime joys will also cause the woman some of her deepest worries and sorrows.

So, too, her relationship with the man is spoilt: 'Your desire shall be for your husband, and he shall rule over you.' At first, this expression is puzzling: the natural desire of a wife for her husband is scarcely a bad thing! Nor (as we have seen) is husbandly authority wrong; it is written into the creation order (2:15-24). What, then, is meant? An important clue is that Genesis uses a similar expression just a few paragraphs later, in 4:7, where God is speaking to Cain. He warns him that '...sin is crouching at the door. Its desire is for you, but you must rule over it.'

In other words, sin desires to master Cain. This suggests that where the expression is used here in 3:16, it is the woman who desires to master the husband. In a landmark article, Susan Foh explained:

> These words mark the beginning of the battle of the sexes. As a result of the fall, man no longer rules easily; he must fight for his headship. Sin has corrupted both the willing submission of the wife and the loving headship of the husband. The woman's desire is to control her husband (to usurp his divinely appointed headship), and he must master her, if he can. So the rule of love founded in paradise is replaced by struggle, tyranny and domination.[4]

The punishment fits the crime. The woman has fallen for the temptation to *be like God, knowing good and evil*. So has her husband. Since both want to be *like God*, each will battle for supremacy. And so we have a very familiar struggle, played out in the ideological conflict between male tyranny (a horrible feature of some cultures and religions) and militant feminism. It doesn't just happen in the political arena: it is expressed in the battles and tensions of countless households.

So a beautiful pattern is now twisted, as in a distorting mirror. There is still much that is beautiful, but things are not as they should be. The husband's responsibility is twisted into chauvinism; the wife's role as 'helper' is seen as weak and demeaning because we have forgotten the divine dignity of serving another and see value only in autonomy. No wonder we now struggle to see the

---

4. Susan Foh, 'What is the woman's desire?' *Westminster Theological Journal* 37 (1974), pp. 376-83; quote from p. 382. Available on the web.

beauty of the original pattern. How far we have now come from the delights of 2:23!

The man comes last: the LORD has most to say to him (17-19), for, strikingly, God regards the final responsibility as his. He has listened to his wife and done what God has forbidden. His sentence falls in the area of his daily work. The *ground* will be cursed; in *pain* (the same word as the woman's pain) he will eat of it; producing food will be a matter of sweaty toil. The farmer's lot will include failed crops, pests, diseases and endless weeding. And you don't need to be a farmer to know what a sweat it can be to put bread on the table: we still have to earn our crust, and we do so amidst broken machinery, workplace politics, failed deliveries, repetitious boredom, crashed computers, jammed copiers, late trains, missed meetings, crossed wires and all the other irritations which put sweat on our shirts each day. Sometimes work will be utterly draining. On a global scale, we find our attempts to control and rule our environment are met with a degree of futility, as our environment produces devastating, unintended effects which backfire on us. Again, in a sense, the punishment fits the crime: the man has eaten what he should not; now eating even what he should eat will be difficult.

And the end of all this will be death.

> By the sweat of your face you shall eat bread, till you return to the ground, for out of it you were taken; for you are dust, and to dust you shall return. (19)

God had said that the result of eating of the tree would be death; now he will keep his word. Man, whose dependence on God has already been stressed by his being made from the ground (2:7), will now be returned to it. Death has come into the world, and the grim reaper will cast his long shadow across all our days as we experience bereavement, illness, ageing, violence and disaster.[5]

Everything is spoilt: our mixed experience of life

Even when we have looked into them, these curses could seem rather arbitrary. Why does the LORD God afflict *these* particular areas of our existence? We have already seen that the punishments seem to fit the crime. But there is something bigger going on, which becomes clear when we look at the structure of the whole of Genesis 2–3. The central part of these two chapters is in fact a mirror image, with *the curses of Genesis 3 going back over the blessings of Genesis 2*. It looks like this:

★Man made from dust (2:7)

   ★Man given luxurious garden to live and work in (2:8-17)

      ★Man and woman one flesh, in harmony (2:18-25)

         ★The crafty serpent (3:1)

            ★THE FALL (3:2-13)

         ★Judgment on the serpent (3:14-15)

      ★Man and woman now at odds (3:16)

   ★Man now sweating and digging out the thistles (3:17-19)

★Man to return to the dust (3:19)

---

5.   See the extra note after this chapter for comments on how we are to understand death coming into the world.

In the curses of Genesis 3, it is as if the movie of Genesis 2 is being played backwards: God takes the woman and the man back through all the good things he has given them, and introduces an element of difficulty into each. This is what accounts for the particular selection of judgments mentioned: they are far from arbitrary. Moreover, the fact that they cover every area of blessing mentioned in chapter two suggests that *every area of our lives has been tarnished in this way*. God does not remove the blessings: there will still be work, marriage and childbirth; there will still be life itself. But each blessing is now spoilt: work becomes toil, marriage will include conflict, childbirth will be painful. The gift of life is still given, but now becomes temporary. Everything is spoilt.

My parents were once out of the house, but received an alarming phone call to say that there had been a fire. They hurried home to find that some workers mending the gas main outside had caused an explosion in the house boiler. The boiler itself was a charred ruin, but the rest of the house seemed all right. Except, that is, for the smoke damage. Smoke had got round the entire place, and now everything smelled of it. On every wall you could wipe your finger to reveal a thin, grimy film; every picture you took down left a non-smoky mark; every item of furniture smelt burnt. Everything was still there, but nothing was now the same. In a similar way, in Genesis 3, God leaves us with the blessings he has given, but each one is damaged; each one has, if you like, a spoilt smell about it.

And isn't life just such a mixed experience? We book that holiday in the sun. It is beautiful, but the brochure never showed us the building site next door, the mosquitoes, the dodgy seafood platter which took the shine off the third night, or the arguments we would have. We spend the last two days of the holiday with a sense of foreboding at the pile of problems which await us on our return. We get back, and with the next pay rise buy a new computer and love the things it can do, but waste frustrating hours sorting out glitches and viruses. We love larking about with our kids, but fret when we hear how unhappy that situation at school has made one of them. We relish the fresh air of the walk in the park, but are weighed down because we must talk about the divorce of good friends. We enjoy the family Christmas, but none of us realize it will be grandpa's last. *In the midst of life, we are in death.*[6]

There is so much blessing, so much to enjoy; but its full enjoyment is at every stage beyond our reach. It is as if between us and total, permanent happiness there exists a great invisible pane of glass: we press our faces against it and long to get through, but cannot. We see the blessings, we enjoy them, but never as we would really like to. And all our enjoyment is cut short by death.

The climax: expulsion (3:20-24)

The climax is dramatic. 'The man called his wife's name Eve, because she was the mother of all living' (as the translators' footnotes tell us, *Eve* sounds like *living*) – and which of us has not followed her example? Then, after providing them with garments of skin, God expels them from the Garden.

> 'Behold, the man has become like one of us in knowing good and evil. Now, lest he reach out his hand and take also of the tree of life and eat, and live for ever

---

6. *The Book of Common Prayer* (1662), Order for the burial of the dead.

–' therefore the LORD God sent him out from the garden of Eden to work the ground from which he was taken. (22-23)

It is intolerable to God that this rebel should gain the immortality that the tree of life promises. The man (and, by implication, also the woman) is to return to the dry land we encountered in Genesis 2:4-7. It is a striking contrast to the abundance of Eden: life here is going to be tough. And the way back is barred, for *cherubim* stand guard. These are fearsome creatures, not the puffy-cheeked figures at the corners of antique maps: and there is *a flaming sword that turned every way to guard the way to the tree of life.* Paradise has been lost.

And with this, there is also the loss of the immediate presence of the LORD God. For, as we saw in Genesis 2, the Garden is God's place, and its delights are the delights of living with him. Now this has gone too: intimacy has been replaced by distance, and access by armed guards. So it is that the most essential relationship to our existence – that between us and our Maker – has been disrupted. And we need to observe that in Genesis 3 this is a *double* disruption. For our part, we have rebelled, and find ourselves hiding from God, avoiding him. But Genesis will not limit our understanding of sin's consequences to the way we distance ourselves from God; he also has distanced us from himself. It is vital to recognize this: for if we want to restore things, it is not just a matter of coming out from behind the trees and saying sorry – however good that may be. No; if God has driven us out of the Garden, then only God can restore us. If there is to be any solution to this desperate situation, *it can only be one that God himself supplies.*

Why? Fitting it all together

How are we to fit all this – the rebellion, the curses and the expulsion – together? What is Genesis wanting us to know?

Most obviously, Genesis is **warning us** that God really is serious when he warns us of the dangers of rebelling against him. The serpent had persuaded Adam and Eve that God was bluffing – 'You will not surely die' (3:4). Now what the serpent said is shown to be a monster lie. God does care, and will judge. The passage shows clearly the fatal error of believing the serpent's account rather than God's.

But, related to this warning, this second half of Genesis 3 is also **explaining the world** to us. Taken together with Genesis 1–2, we have here an enormously significant explanation for the bafflingly mixed-up world we live in. On the one hand, we live in a creation which still proclaims the glory of God. On the other, our enjoyment of it is at every point spoiled and limited – and this Genesis traces back up the river of time to God's sentence on human rebellion. A single word, *because*, sums it up: 'And to Adam he said, Because you have...' (3:17). We live in a world made by a majestic Creator – but things have gone wrong between us and him.[7]

Indeed, with Genesis in our hands, we can go further and say that God has seen to it that our experience in life is a constant reminder of these two great truths – God's majesty as revealed by creation, and the fact that there is

---

7. Of course – and it is vitally important that we say this – Genesis is not explaining the details of this at an individual level. It is not saying why this tragedy happens to this family, while that family seems fine. We cannot, and must not, try to answer that ourselves: the LORD himself ticked off Job's 'comforters' for seeking to explain his illness as a divine judgment for some particular sin (Job 42:7). Rather, Genesis is speaking at a general level, about the whole human race.

a problem between us and him. For all the areas singled out here have in common the fact that they are highly visible in our day-to-day lives. It is as if God wanted, through these things, to keep on insisting to us, as a race, that all is not well between us and him. We cannot physically see the disruption in our relationship with God, so God makes it known by these effects, shouting to us that there is a problem. They are, in a sense, as C. S. Lewis famously put it when talking about suffering, 'God's megaphone to rouse a deaf world'.[8]

Speaking personally, I know I need the megaphone. We are so used to rebellion as a way of life that we might not think the problem between us and God is serious, were it not for the heavy burden of futility and suffering we must live under. I might never take God's promise of future judgment – often reiterated by Jesus – seriously, were it not for the fact that already, in day-to-day life, I see the outworking of his judgment in Genesis 3, and recognize that the true and living God means business.

We could think of it this way. People have long wrestled with the problem of pain: Why does a good and all-powerful God allow suffering in the world he has made? It is a profound and difficult question, with many dimensions, and we can easily find ourselves shying away from it. But perhaps *this is the very question God wants us to ask.* He has shaped our daily experience to press the question upon us, so that we might find the answer Genesis gives: that, as a race, all is not well between us and our Creator. He has done this so that we might seek him for the solution he has provided.

---

8. C. S. Lewis, *The Problem of Pain* (this edition, Glasgow: Collins, 1977), p. 81.

Three notes of hope

For God has a solution. Grim though this section of Genesis is, there are some fascinating clues that suggest that though Paradise has been lost, this is not the end of the story. We cannot get ourselves out of this mess, but God has a plan.

For one thing, God clearly signals that all is not over for the human race. Did you notice a surprise underlying the whole passage? In 2:17, God had warned them about the tree of the knowledge of good and evil, 'in the day that you eat of it you shall surely die.' If that was all we knew, we might expect that shortly after they had eaten it, that would be the end for Adam and Eve. The story would be finished. But it is not. Certainly, death now comes – but not immediately. Throughout his words to the woman and the man, the assumption is that the human race will continue. God was not bluffing when he spoke of death, but he has not given up on humanity yet. He does not pronounce their ultimate doom, as he does for the serpent. Indeed, he treats them with kindness: in 3:21, he provides for them *garments of skins*, appropriate for the new world in which they will find themselves.[9] The relationship with God has been disrupted, but he is still their God, and will still provide for them.

Secondly, there is a hint that God wants the rebels back. We have already seen in 3:9 that God's very first words after the Fall are *Where are you?* – indeed, this is the very first question God asks humanity in the Bible. Of course, he does so partly because he wants to confront them with what they have done; but surely we are right also to hear him asking because he wants them back. I remember,

---

9. Many commentators have pointed out that since the provision of skins required the death of animals, here is the first hint of the great system of sacrificial provision which God, in his grace, would provide.

when I was very young and at primary school, hearing similar words. It was a parents' event. I thought it would be fun to hide under a table in the corner of a classroom. I hadn't realized that a missing child isn't always great fun for parents who care! As they went round calling for me, they were not altogether pleased – but it was first and foremost because they wanted me back. God's searching on this occasion hints at a greater search and rescue, which will be the story of the whole Bible. When, in Luke's Gospel, we hear Jesus say that 'the Son of Man came to seek and to save the lost', we are hearing an echo of the very first question God asks man in the Bible.

Thirdly, there is just a hint of how things will be restored. Tucked away in the curse on the serpent (3:15) comes a remarkable promise:

> 'I will put enmity between you and the woman, and between your offspring and her offspring; he shall bruise your head, and you shall bruise his heel.'

While this may be taken as a general prediction of hostilities between future people and serpents, the bruising of the serpent's *head* suggests a blow that is ultimately lethal, administered by the woman's offspring. So from this point on in the Bible's story, we are beginning to look for this great victory, and wonder who will achieve it. It is no exaggeration to say that all the Old Testament's hopes, expressed in so many ways, of a Great Rescuer who will come, start here. When, at the end of his letter to the Romans, the Apostle Paul can assure his readers that 'The God of peace will soon crush Satan under your feet',[10] he is surely echoing this very first promise of the Christian gospel in the Bible: and he does so with confidence

---

10. Romans 16:20

because he is looking back to One who, at enormous personal cost ('you shall bruise his heel'), came to undo the devil's evil work. Doesn't our day-to-day experience make us long for that?

There is a word that Genesis has not yet used: the word *grace*. But we are already encountering the concept, in the very character of God. Despite the disaster of the Fall, the story is not over. God carries on, God cares and God is planning a rescue. In our daily experience, he is urging us to seek that. Will you?

EXTRA NOTE: THE PHYSICAL EFFECTS OF THE FALL

In what sense did the Fall cause death to come into the world? The question is vigorously debated, particularly by those seeking to tease out the relationship between Genesis and scientific discovery. Some say that the 'death' that came was only spiritual; it was Adam's relationship with God that was broken. Others claim that all death, human and animal, follows the Fall and is a result of it. As is so often the case in 'Genesis debates', we need to see both what Scripture says and what it does not say. Extrapolations from Scripture should not be confused with Scripture itself. The following brief notes do not answer the question, but rather are intended to let Genesis give us a steer as we ponder the issues.

1. A straightforward reading of Genesis 3:19 indicates that the kind of death God sentences man to is physical:

> 'By the sweat of your face you shall eat bread, till you return to the ground, for out of it you were taken; for you are dust, and to dust you shall return.'

Although in the Bible the word *death* can mean more than physical death, the emphasis on *dust* implies that the death in mind here is, at least, physical.

2. Only human death is mentioned in this way. Nothing is said about death in the animal kingdom. Again, in Romans 5, where Paul discusses the Fall and death, only human death is in view. The Apostle writes:

> Therefore, just as sin came into the world through one man, and death through sin, and so death spread to all men because all sinned... [11]

We should not be too quick, therefore, to say that all animal death is the result of the Fall. On the contrary, some Scripture passages marvel at predation. In Psalm 104, the entire content of which (except the final verse!) is a celebration of God's power and provision in creation, 'The young lions roar for their prey, seeking their food from God.'[12] Likewise, Job's hawk 'spies out the prey... His young ones suck up blood.'[13] If we find ourselves considering predation an evil, we need to ask ourselves if our squeamishness comes from the Bible or from twenty-first-century sentimentality.[14]

3. We are not told exactly how this death comes about. All we are told is that the eating of the tree of life is what was barred to humanity as God's sentence on rebellion (3:22).

---

11. Romans 5:12

12. Psalm 104:21; see also John Calvin's comments on this Psalm.

13. Job 39:28-29

14. Isaiah 11:6-7 certainly paints a picture of a future in harmony. But as Collins has argued, 'this may be a figurative description of the peaceful reign brought in by the Messiah'. (C. J. Collins: *Science and Faith* [Wheaton: Crossway, 2003], p. 157). Note that this vision of the future also includes meaty meals: Isaiah 25:6.

4. When Genesis 1:31 says that all God had made was *very good*, again, it does not define that. So we must be careful not to impose our own categories of what *very good* looks like (no meat-eating by crocodiles, no storm winds, etc.). Indeed, the creation mandate in 1:28 explicitly includes subduing the world, and this can be taken to imply that the world had a certain 'wildness' about it, as created. This is the world – different from Eden – to which the man and woman are returned in 3:23. There is as much of an 'inside Eden / outside Eden' contrast as there is a 'before / after' in the narrative.

5. The world needs its ruler: humanity. We see this both in 1:28 and 2:5. With humanity in rebellion, the whole creation will suffer. Derek Kidner memorably comments on the disruption caused by the Fall:

> This multiple disarray is, from one aspect, his punishment, pronounced by God; from another, it is the plain outcome of his anarchy. Leaderless, the choir of creation can only grind on in discord.[15]

No wonder the whole of creation groans – and longs *for the sons of God to be revealed*, for then it will be properly ruled.[16]

6. In the end, we are simply not told exactly how, physically speaking, the connection between the Fall and human death and suffering works. We are simply told it is a reality – for the Bible's businesslike

---

15. Kidner, *Genesis*, p. 73.
16. Romans 8:19-22

focus is always on what we need to know, rather than what we might like to know. Powerful though the desire to speculate is, the wise will not go beyond what is written.[17]

---

17.   1 Corinthians 4:6

GENESIS 4:1-16

[1]Now Adam knew Eve his wife, and she conceived and bore Cain, saying, 'I have produced a man with the help of the LORD.' [2]And again, she bore his brother Abel. Now Abel was a keeper of sheep, and Cain a worker of the ground. [3]In the course of time Cain brought to the LORD an offering of the fruit of the ground, [4]and Abel also brought of the firstborn of his flock and of their fat portions. And the LORD had regard for Abel and his offering, [5]but for Cain and his offering he had no regard. So Cain was very angry, and his face fell. [6]The LORD said to Cain, 'Why are you angry, and why has your face fallen? [7]If you do well, will you not be accepted? And if you do not do well, sin is crouching at the door. Its desire is for you, but you must rule over it.'

[8]Cain spoke to Abel his brother. And when they were in the field, Cain rose up against his brother Abel and killed him. [9]Then the LORD said to Cain, 'Where is Abel your brother?' He said, 'I do not know; am I my brother's keeper?' [10]And the LORD said, 'What have you done? The voice of your brother's blood is crying to me from the ground. [11]And now you are cursed from the ground, which has opened its mouth to receive your brother's blood from your hand. [12]When you work the ground, it shall no longer yield to you its strength. You shall be a fugitive and a wanderer on the earth.' [13]Cain said to the LORD, 'My punishment is greater than I can bear. [14]Behold, you have driven me today away from the ground, and from your face I shall be hidden. I shall be a fugitive and a wanderer on the earth, and whoever finds me will kill me.' [15]Then the LORD said to him, 'Not so! If anyone kills Cain, vengeance shall be taken on him sevenfold.' And the LORD put a mark on Cain, lest any who found him should attack him. [16]Then Cain went away from the presence of the LORD and settled in the land of Nod, east of Eden.

13

Blood on the ground
Genesis 4:1-16

What happened next? What will life be like, in a world which has rejected its Maker? Genesis 4 begins the answer. Although it lies outside the tight mirror-image structure of chapters 2–3, it is very much part of this section: it comes before the next major divide in the book (5:1). Genesis does not want us to wait before facing the facts.

God's persistent grace (4:1-2)
The first piece of news is good:

> Now Adam knew Eve his wife, and she conceived and bore Cain, saying, 'I have gotten a man with the help of the LORD.' (Gen. 4:1)[1]

Eve has a boy, and she is thrilled. Could this be the serpent-crusher of 3:15? The boy's very name – Cain – sounds similar in Hebrew to *brought forth* or *acquired,* and stresses the significance of what has happened. And she

---

1.   Readers of British English will prefer 'I have gained'.

knows that it is with the LORD's help this has happened. Then little Abel follows (2).

None of this may seem so remarkable to us. The antenatal wards are always busy. But pause and remember the circumstances: these births come after all that has gone on! Adam and Eve have rejected God's authority, and been thrown out of the Garden. But still he perseveres with them. We saw, in Genesis 3, the notes of hope, and that God clearly has a future for the human race, in spite of everything. Here it is confirmed. He is persistent in his grace.

My parents-in-law once invited a distinguished couple to dinner. But due to a mix-up about the date, the guests mistakenly arrived 24 hours early. There they were, smartly dressed, on the doorstep, while their hosts were in casual mode and quite unprepared. Fortunately, everyone had a sense of humour, and they all had a happy evening. But my in-laws' surprise that evening was nothing to what they felt the following evening when – yes – the doorbell rang again! The same people, the right date. 'Us again!', they announced cheerfully. The guests had, very correctly, honoured their commitment to come when originally agreed! They were, one might say, persistent. They stuck to the original plan. Here in Genesis 4, God is being persistent. He is keeping to his plan for humanity that we might 'be fruitful and multiply' (1:28). The LORD is not defeated by human sin; he will have his way.

Rage against God (4:2-5)

The next we hear, the boys have grown up. Abel is now a pastoral farmer, while Cain's speciality is arable (2). In Genesis 3–4, we read that each brings offerings to the

LORD: Cain some of his crop and Abel from his flock. And the puzzle is that the LORD reacts differently to each: he 'had regard for Abel and his offering, but for Cain and his offering he had no regard' (4).

Why does God take this view? It is not immediately obvious. Perhaps it is because somehow a meat offering is more acceptable to him than a grain offering, anticipating the sacrificial system, which had at its heart the death of an animal. Or perhaps there is a hint that Abel was being more generous when he brought *the firstborn of his flock and some of their fat portions*, in contrast to his brother who merely *brought to the LORD an offering of the fruit of the ground*, as if he were merely giving God a tip. That may be an implied warning to us about our attitude to God. But I doubt we can press this point, because Genesis doesn't. The focus is simply on the fact that, somehow, Abel's offering is pleasing to God and Cain's is not. Abel is living the LORD's way, but his brother chooses not to.

There is a significant point here. In our arrogance, we can easily think that God *has* to be pleased with whatever we offer him. But that is no better in reality than the person who insists on giving you black coffee with two sugars when, in fact, you want white with none! Even this early in the Bible, we are encountering the vital truth that the true God is to be approached, and served, only his way. It is a truth that will run and run: it is there in Exodus, where the LORD gives Moses the instructions for making the Tabernacle (the special tent where God meets his people), insisting that it follows exactly the pattern God has shown Moses.[2] It culminates

---

2.   Exodus 25:9, 40

in the central New Testament truth that only through Jesus can we come to God. In his own words: 'I am the way, and the truth, and the life. No one comes to the Father except through me.'[3]

Now how do you react to that? Cain's response was rage:

> So Cain was very angry, and his face fell.

Of course. In our pride, there is nothing which irks us more than the suggestion that we cannot ourselves set the terms of approach to God, or decide for ourselves how we will live. Here is the anger which says, 'Why isn't my way acceptable to you?' It's an argument, at root, about who is God: him or us. Are we free to set the terms, or is he? The issue is at its most emotive when religion is involved. 'Isn't my way of doing religion enough? How dare you say it isn't?' Abel has found out what pleases the LORD, but Cain presses on in proud independence. The suggestion that he needs to live for God is hateful.

Not the serpent, but sin (4:6-7)
At this point, the LORD speaks.

> 'Why are you angry, and why has your face fallen? If you do well, will you not be accepted? And if you do not do well, sin is crouching at the door. Its desire is for you, but you must rule over it.' (6-7)

God is showing Cain a way back. The offer is on the table. Here is the LORD's persistent grace again! He is not writing Cain off; it is not yet too late. The Great Evangelist speaks.

---

3. John 14:6

But if Cain will not listen, *sin is crouching at the door. Its desire is for you...* Do you notice the new element in the story? This is the first occurrence in the Bible of the word *sin*. Of course, it's not the first occurrence of the concept – that was introduced most plainly in Genesis 3 – but there is a significant difference at this point. Cain's parents had been tempted by something *outside* them, the serpent. But this is no longer external. The temptation is now right *at the door*. In some horrible way, the rebellious attitude the serpent commended in the Garden has now gained access to Cain's very nature. How exactly this has happened, we are not told. But it is hard not to see a strange appropriateness in the link between Cain and his parents, the first rebels, the link emphasized by his name, *Brought Forth*.

Very strikingly, sin is personified. It is pictured as a kind of monster, *crouching at the door*. It *desires to have you*. It is more than a force; it has become so absorbed into the self that it has acquired personality. Sin has bonded itself on to Cain's motives, ideas and attitudes: it moves him, speaks to him, wants to master him. And Genesis is holding up a mirror to us, too. In the account of how he came from atheism to Christian faith, *Surprised by Joy*, C. S. Lewis tells of how, shortly before his conversion, he began to think about his own character.

> For the first time I examined myself with a seriously practical purpose. And there I found what appalled me; a zoo of lusts, a bedlam of ambitions, a nursery of fears, a harem of fondled hatreds. My name was legion.[4]

In our better moments, don't we realize that this is so? We have thoughts which are thoroughly shameful – and yet

---

4. C. S. Lewis, *Surprised by Joy* (Bles, 1955, reprinted by Fount, London, 1977) p. 181.

they are *our* thoughts! Often, as in Cain's case, it is only the Word of God which really alerts us to the presence of this evil. To follow its impulses must bring disaster.

The first martyr (4:8)

Cain ignores God's warning. What happens next is told with chilling economy:

> Cain spoke to Abel his brother. And when they were in the field, Cain rose up against his brother Abel and killed him. (8)

The crime has a premeditated feel about it: it happens out in the field, where no one can see. We are not told how one brother killed another, but what we can say is that we are only in the fourth chapter of the Bible and already there is a murder. Twice we have the word *brother,* emphasizing the horror of the crime. How far we have now travelled from the blissful world of Eden!

The obvious question is: Why did Cain kill Abel? We might speculate that the motive is envy: that would be a good guess, given that God had accepted Abel's sacrifice but not Cain's. There may be truth there. But I doubt that this will do as a full explanation. For one thing, the LORD offers Cain a way out; if it were envy, it could easily be relieved. More importantly, the text itself never gives envy as a motive. All Genesis does say, quite simply, is that Abel's sacrifice is acceptable, and Cain's isn't. Abel lives God's way, and Cain doesn't.

Is that enough, on its own, to explain the murder? I think so. If you are seeking to live in God's world your way and not his, as Cain was, what could be worse than having a brother who is living God's way? Abel is accepted by God and devoted to God; he is, to Cain, an ongoing, visible reminder of how he ought to be living. And Cain hates it. He does not want to live God's way. He wants to wipe God out of the picture. He can't, of course; but he can get rid of God's man. His brother must die. Cain's rebellion against God is in itself the motive for the murder of his brother.

The Apostle John explains Abel's death this way, too.

> We should not be like Cain, who was of the evil one and murdered his brother. And why did he murder him? Because his own deeds were evil and his brother's righteous.[5]

It was simply that; Genesis gives no further explanation, for none is required. But there is an important lesson: 'Do not be surprised, brothers, that the world hates you.'[6] A world which chooses to walk away from God will always oppose his followers. They always have, as Jesus reminded the scribes and Pharisees in the A–Z history lesson he gave them: '...from the blood of innocent Abel to the blood of Zechariah the son of Barachiah...'[7] If you own the name of Jesus, you can expect a measure of the same treatment.

In the West, we don't get too much of this, perhaps because society is fairly indifferent to Christian faith, or prizes tolerance. There is the occasional snide remark and a bit of mockery, and sometimes a measure of ostracism. In some other parts of the world, however, it is quite different, and many thousands each year suffer the same fate as Abel.

---

5. 1 John 3:12

6. 1 John 3:13

7. Matthew 23:35

In a world which rebels against God, this is what happens to God's man (or woman). And, even this early in the Bible, this puts a chilling thought into our heads: *if this is what happens to God's man, what on earth would happen if God himself were to come into the world?* What would men do to him?

The blood that condemns (4:9-10)

No sooner is the deed done than the LORD speaks to Cain:

> 'Where is Abel your brother?' (9)

There is an echo of the LORD's question in the Garden, 'Where are you?' (3:8), except that this time there is someone dead. Cain replies, as his parents had, by denying responsibility:

> 'I do not know; am I my brother's keeper?' (4:9).

It's nothing to do with me! But God will not be fobbed off; he never is.

> 'What have you done? The voice of your brother's blood is crying to me from the ground.' (10)

The LORD has seen exactly what has happened. Nothing in all creation is hidden from his sight. There is blood on the ground, forensic evidence of the crime. John Calvin memorably comments:

> Abel was speechless when his throat was being cut, or in whatever other manner he was losing his life; but after his death the voice of his blood was more vehement than any eloquence of the orator.[8]

---

8.   J. Calvin, *Commentary on Genesis* (1563, Translated by J. King, 1847, Reprinted by Baker Book House, Grand Rapids, 1996), p. 207.

The ground cries out to God on Abel's behalf, and God sees it.

Thank God that he does. Thank God that the death of an innocent person cannot be hidden from him; that he hears the cry of the murdered unborn. Thank God that he knows when his people suffer, even if it never makes it into the media. For their blood cries out to him, even in a world where many, quite literally, get away with murder. In God's world, ultimately there will always be justice.

But if the crimson stain cries out on Abel's behalf, it also cries out against Cain. The blood speaks of his guilt. Did you notice in the passage the curious emphasis on *the ground*? 'The voice of your brother's blood is crying to me from the ground.' The blood-stained ground will speak of his guilt.

Now at this stage, Genesis must make us think, rather uncomfortably, about ourselves. For, like the stained ground, the world about each of us has a way of recording our guilt. Our damaged physical environment bears grim witness to our greed. Our lives leave other trails behind them: in people's memories, in bank statements, tax returns, criminal records, browser histories, in emails sitting on someone else's computer. There is the faded photo of the elderly relative we neglected; the exaggerated expense claim, the child wounded by cruelty, the colleague whose career has been damaged by our speculative gossip. Quite apart from the guilt we feel when we see these reminders, don't they all cry out to a holy God? That is the emphasis here, for God says 'The voice of your brother's blood is crying *to me* from the ground.' The question is not what we feel, but what God sees. Our guilt is not simply an emotion, but an objective reality before God the judge.

Like Cain, we try to deny our wrongdoing and its consequences. We claim to have no responsibility for that person. Or we widen our excuses: we assure ourselves that a feeling of guilt is just a morbid mindset; we redefine sin, saying our action was not wrong; we cheaply and arrogantly assume God's forgiveness; we even deny there's a God to whom we are accountable at all. But there is a God – who sees. We have already learnt from Genesis 3 that he will not ignore human wickedness.

The unbearable nature of God's sentence (4:11-16)

The LORD now pronounces sentence:

> 'And now you are cursed from the ground, which has opened its mouth to receive your brother's blood from your hand. When you work the ground, it shall no longer yield to you its strength.' (11-12a)

It's as if the ground will now be less fruitful for Cain because it has been contaminated by this terrible crime. Polluted by the murder, the ground will be cursed. The soil, which had brought forth life, now speaks of death, and will not yield its best to him. Instead, it will call 'Guilty! Guilty!', and Cain will become 'a fugitive and a wanderer on the earth' (12b).

Cain sees the gravity of his situation:

> 'My punishment is greater than I can bear. Behold, you have driven me today away from the ground, and from your face I shall be hidden. I shall be a fugitive and

a wanderer on the earth, and whoever finds me will kill me.' (13-14)

He sees how wretched it will be to be driven from the land; but, even more, to be hidden from God's face. And that makes him fear for the future: does he already anticipate some kind of revenge killing? Is he now concerned that he will be quite beyond God's care?

In his extraordinary grace, God promises to put a mark on Cain to protect him – but only by the threat of further vengeance, for, it seems, this is the only language the human heart will now understand. Even after Cain's most heinous deed, God is still protecting this man. If we saw God's grace at the start of Genesis 4, in the continuation of the human race, how much more do we see it here!

Yet that gracious mark that God puts on Cain does not solve the problem of his guilt. The past is not erased, and God's sentence does fall on the murderer:

Cain went away from the presence of the LORD and settled in the land of Nod, east of Eden. (16)

The picture is of alienation from God, and a life of restlessness. Cain is distanced from God's presence (literally his *face*) and further from Eden (his place). His new abode is not fixed: it is *Nod*, which means 'wandering'. It is, in a sense, a foretaste of the terrible reality Jesus spoke about when he talked about hell.[9] When Cain said, 'My punishment is greater than I can bear'(13), our English versions of the Bible remind us in the footnotes that the word translated *punishment* also means *guilt*. Perhaps Thomas Cranmer, the architect of

9.   Matthew 25:41; Mark 9: 42-48; Luke 16:19-31; see also Romans 2:5.

the English *Book of Common Prayer*, had these words of Cain's in mind when he expressed the way we should feel when we face the stains on our consciences: 'The remembrance of them is grievous unto us; the burden of them is intolerable.'[10] So a question: in the face of a holy God, who will call us to account, and in the face of our sins, the evidence of which cries out to him, what would be the most beautiful word in the world?

Surely there can only be one: FORGIVENESS.

The blood that speaks a better word

How can forgiveness be found? This turns out to be the great pressing question that runs from here on through Scripture, and it is a question which will rightly concern any self-aware person. Genesis 4 gives us no answer – but the story of Cain and Abel is picked up in a New Testament passage that does. It picks up the same theme of *blood*, first mentioned here in Genesis (and then developed in the Old Testament sacrificial system).

The answer comes through a man who is in some ways quite similar to Abel. Thousands of years later, there is another murder, of another innocent man – God's man, hated for his righteous deeds. Here is more blood, spattered on to the ground. But this time, the blood belongs to God's only Son, and it is dripping from a wooden cross. The writer of the letter to the Hebrews tells his readers that this is how, for them, the problem of guilt has been solved:

> You have come.... to Jesus, the mediator of a new covenant, and to the sprinkled blood that speaks a better word than the blood of Abel.[11]

10. *Book of Common Prayer* (1662), Confession in the order for the Lord's Supper.

11. Hebrews 12:22-24

Here is blood that *speaks a better word*. When God saw Abel's blood, it shouted to him 'guilty!'. But when God saw Jesus' blood, it shouted to him 'not guilty' – on our behalf! For Christ died in our place, bearing the punishment we deserve, for our sins. He died that we might be forgiven. All who have gone to him for refuge can look to that cross, and remember those stains of blood, which say of our sin, 'All gone'.

I met a man who told me how, years before, he had been pilfering army property. He woke in the night, terrified by what he had done: he knew he had to find forgiveness. This was how he came to faith in Christ. He told me how he had heard what Christ had done, and brought his guilt to him. He found forgiveness, and life, and health, and peace – and because of the change of his own heart that went with that, he confessed what he had done to his employers. His restless wandering ended.

In the gruesome account of Cain and Abel, Genesis is showing us what life will look like in a world that is rebelling against its Creator. It is also introducing the word *sin*, and, particularly, making us face up to the two terrible problems it brings: its power (*its desire is for you*) and its guilt (*Your brother's blood is crying to me from the ground.*). How are we to find an answer to either? Genesis does not say; but instead, it is pointing us to the personal and absolute necessity of the solution God would one day provide in Christ.

> *Rock of ages, cleft for me,*
> *Let me hide myself in thee.*
> *Let the water and the blood,*
> *From Thy riven side which flowed,*
> *Be of sin the double cure*
> *Cleanse me from its guilt and power.*[12]

---

12. Hymn 'Rock of Ages' by A.M. Toplady (1763).

GENESIS 4:17-26

¹⁷Cain knew his wife, and she conceived and bore Enoch. When he built a city, he called the name of the city after the name of his son, Enoch. ¹⁸To Enoch was born Irad, and Irad fathered Mehujael, and Mehujael fathered Methushael, and Methushael fathered Lamech. ¹⁹And Lamech took two wives. The name of one was Adah, and the name of the other Zillah. ²⁰Adah bore Jabal; he was the father of those who dwell in tents and have livestock. ²¹His brother's name was Jubal; he was the father of all those who play the lyre and pipe. ²²Zillah also bore Tubal-cain; he was the forger of all instruments of bronze and iron. The sister of Tubal-cain was Naamah.

²³Lamech said to his wives:

'Adah and Zillah, hear my voice;
  you wives of Lamech, listen to what I say:
I have killed a man for wounding me,
  a young man for striking me.
²⁴If Cain's revenge is sevenfold,
  then Lamech's is seventy-sevenfold.'

²⁵And Adam knew his wife again, and she bore a son and called his name Seth, for she said, 'God has appointed for me another offspring instead of Abel, for Cain killed him.' ²⁶To Seth also a son was born, and he called his name Enosh. At that time people began to call upon the name of the LORD.

14 Our only hope
Genesis 4:17-26

There was good news all over that morning's papers. London had just won its bid to host the 2012 Olympics. As they sat on the Underground, heading to work, many Londoners were relishing the prospect of seeing the world's greatest sporting event come to their own city.

But also on the trains were three terrorists. At 8:50 a.m., deep underground, each simultaneously detonated a peroxide-based rucksack bomb to create three huge explosions. An hour later, up on the surface, a double-decker bus was ripped apart by a fourth bomb. It was 7 July 2005, since known in the U.K. as 7/7. Fifty-two people were killed and 700 injured. The papers the next day were an astonishing contrast to the day before. Gone were the pictures of celebrating crowds; now there were pages and pages of haunting images of survivors wrapped in bandages.

That Sunday at church, we turned to the Bible to make sense of this bewildering juxtaposition of events. I held up the two newspaper front pages: the first, of the jubilant crowds hearing about the Olympics; the second, the next day, of casualties and broken glass. How could the world be such a mixed-up place, with triumph and tragedy on successive days? Where are we to find hope in such a mess?

We looked up this final part of Genesis 4. That may seem like a strangely obscure text for a sermon; but this passage confronts us again with the mixed-up world in which we live. Most importantly, it draws this section of Genesis to a conclusion by showing us why, when men '...began to call up on the name of the LORD', they were following the only realistic course of action in the face of a world like ours.

Progress and human genius (4:17-22)

Cain has murdered Abel, and is driven further from the presence of the LORD, but God's purposes for him are not extinguished. Still God's grace persists (amazingly), and the line continues. Cain and his wife have Enoch, and a city is being built.[1] Indeed, after several more generations, things are beginning to look distinctly promising. For here – fifth down the line from Cain – comes Lamech, the man with the brilliant family. Look at their boys!

[Jabal] was the father of those who dwell in tents and have livestock. His brother's name was Jubal; he was the father of all those who play the lyre and pipe. (20-21)

Then there was Tubal-Cain:

... he was the forger of all instruments of bronze and iron. (22)

---

1. Genesis gives no direct answer to the old question of where Cain got his wife from, any more than it tells us who the city was for. Some have suggested that these are clues within Genesis that the account is a spotlight, and there is more going on than it is the author's purpose to tell us. But we simply don't know.

Farming, culture and technology – all in one family! Think of those circular letters people send at Christmas, often with news of their children's achievements: imagine what Lamech and the wives would have said about theirs! And that's not to mention daughter Naamah.

Here we have the beginnings of human civilization, which archaeological evidence traces to the very area in view: the ancient Middle East. We see here some early developments in the extraordinary ability of the human race to farm, develop arts and culture, and invent world-changing technology. It is all part of the awesome ability that goes with being made *in the image of God*; it is an expression of our delegated rule over God's world.

More than that, the idea of *father of...* here implies a step forward, or what we would call progress. This generation was further on than their predecessors. That is our experience, too. In only just over a century, we have had manned flight, antibiotics, computers, telecoms, plastics, genetic engineering, cars, supermarkets, movies, recorded music, the web. Agricultural technology has given us miracle rice and the green revolution, and medicine, huge advances in life expectancy. Even progress itself accelerates: the phone in your pocket today has more memory than a mainframe computer thirty years ago. At every Olympic Games, new records are set, as new training regimes push the limits of human physical performance. We wonder what wonders our children will live to see.

Here, then, is marvellous progress – even in Cain's family, a family that shows no sign of interest in the living God. (This, incidentally, is why it is wrong to dismiss the results of scientific enquiry conducted by the irreligious: there is no reason why they cannot uncover the truth and do good science.) With such progress on different fronts, the future is looking bright for this family.

Until dad comes in.

Sin and human brutality (4:23-24)

Just after hearing of the boys' achievements, there is a most unpleasant little bit of poetry, in Genesis 4:23-24. Perhaps it's in verse because Lamech so relishes what he has to say. He comes in and boasts to his wives of the way he has killed a young man who has somehow injured him. He doesn't explain the circumstances (Was it an accident? Was it an attack?), but what he delights in is the ferocity of his revenge. Lamech is a man not to be messed with; this one did, and it was the end of him. Cain may have had a mark on him which meant that the one who attacked him paid seven times over, but with Lamech you get much more. For Lamech is Mr Big: he is centre of his world, and no one had better challenge that.

Lamech is not so far from each of us. When we read of a road-rage attack, we shake our heads in disapproval, but have we not felt that anger well up inside us when someone cuts us up on the road? When our standing has been threatened by some insult, or when we feel we have been treated with less importance than we deserve, have we not dwelt on the desire to find the most damaging barb with which to respond? It is there in us all. Here is the individual who is so talented, yet whose life, again and again, is a moral failure. Here is the brilliant family, who can't get on with each other. Here is the rock band that inevitably busts up. Here is our own heart: our finest achievements blemished by what lies within us And what a let-down it is: all this talent in the family, and now this! Here we have it, all in the same family: brilliant talent alongside brutality, vindictiveness and cruelty.

Moreover, the pattern of this family is also the pattern of world history. If the past hundred years brought us all those wonderful advances, it also brought 'The war to end all wars', closely followed by the second; it saw the Holocaust, Hiroshima, Korea, Vietnam, Sudan, Iraq (three times), Cambodia's 'killing fields', Rwanda, Srebrenica, 9/11, Afghanistan, 7/7, Libya, Syria and more. It has been estimated that more people died in wars in the twentieth century than in all the previous centuries combined. Our vocabulary now routinely includes words such as genocide, suicide bomber, insurgency and roadside bomb.

I had, in fact, preached on this passage before 7/7; I had used it also for the last Sunday of 1999. What could we look forward to as we peered into the twenty-first century? More of this mixture, suggests Genesis 4. Twenty-one months later, terrorists flew planes into the World Trade Center and the Pentagon. What could speak more eloquently of human progress than a jet airliner, in all its astounding sophistication, and those magnificent buildings? But what could speak more of human brutality than deliberately to fly them, loaded with passengers, into offices full of people?

Genesis has already shown us the cause of all this. We are made in the image of God, but we have rejected him, and want to live as rulers of our own lives. It is true that there has been great progress all through human history, but the human heart remains as stubbornly sinful as it was in Genesis 4. There have been thousands of years of progress in all areas, and not an inch of movement on human nature.

The realism of Genesis (no misplaced optimism!)

The sequence of the account is important. Progress comes first, then brutality. Our hopes are raised, then dashed. Surely Genesis (which, as we have seen, uses sequence to make points) does this deliberately. For such is the power and success of much human achievement that it cons us into thinking that we can dig ourselves out of every hole. That is the very point at which Genesis gives us an icy blast of reality. It is not that we should regret progress. Nor should we stop pursuing it, for it is often true that we can do much good. But, in the end, Genesis is showing us that we cannot solve our biggest, deepest problems.

The Victorians were great believers in progress. 'Progress' (with a capital P) was the theme of the 1851 Great Exhibition. Some Victorian anthropologists developed a three-stage model of development in human cultures: from savagery through barbarism to civilization. The trouble with this scheme is, of course, knowing where to put Lamech and his family!

Every election, the politicians present themselves as the answer. Any of us who are fortunate enough to live in a democracy should be glad we have the vote, but the truth is that we will be disappointed, for no government can deal with human nature. Education will not deal with it (useful though it is); nor will more money in the economy (excellent though it is to work against poverty). Better science and technology cannot fix it. Nor will some new political ideology: as Helmut Thielicke perceptively observes, 'As a rule, those who have promised men a heaven on earth have made of life a hell.'[2] For at the heart of the human problem is the problem of the human heart.

If we have a grain of honesty, we know this in our own lives. We put hope in our talents, but again and again our character proves the fly in the ointment. We look for fulfilment, but our worst enemy is ourselves.

So is there an answer? There is just a clue, at the very end of Genesis 4.

Calling on the name of the LORD (4:25-26)

There is rejoicing in Adam's household: Eve has another boy, Seth. She sees him as a kind of replacement for murdered Abel, and there may be special significance in this. For Abel was righteous; he was God's man, as we have seen. Now, from Seth comes Enosh, and the beginnings of another line, also of those who lived God's way. For it was at this time that *people began to call on the name of the LORD.*[3]

We would love to know more – no details are given – but Genesis has surely placed this here for a reason. Might it not be to point us to the only way we can go, in answer to our human problem? For we have run out of other options.

Consider all we have seen in Genesis. Isn't this ancient book preaching to us that calling on the name of

2. Helmut Thielicke, *How the World Began* (London: James Clarke, 1964), p. 181.

3. It was only later, in Exodus 3, that the meaning of the LORD's name was revealed. Genesis' point is that it was this God, the God of Eden, the God of the Bible, to whom they called.

the LORD – this God, the Creator, the God of Genesis – is the only answer? In Genesis 1, he was introduced to us as Creator. If so, surely relating to him is only right and natural? Indeed, we also saw a hint right at the beginning, in 1:3, that he is the one who can sort out the mess. Genesis 2 showed us that being with him is the place of real human flourishing. In Genesis 3, we saw that the root of our problems lay in rebellion against him. In chapter four, we have seen the double problem of the human race: the guilt of sin, and the power of sin. Before a holy God, we urgently need forgiveness, lest, like Cain, we be banished from his presence. And in Lamech's family we are confronted with the problem of human nature. None of this, Genesis has shown us, we can sort for ourselves. Instead, we are to look to God: to *call on the name of the LORD*. In Western society it is not trendy to look in the direction Seth's family looked. But Genesis compels us to do so: it has closed off all other options.

What does it mean, for us today, to *call on the name of the LORD*? It means to call on Jesus Christ. It is right to say this, even though Genesis was written so long before him. For this genealogy – beginning here in Genesis 4 and running through those mysterious family trees later in Genesis, and beyond – is pointing to someone. After Adam, Seth; after Seth, Enosh... whose family tree will this be? Luke's Gospel, in chapter 3, gives us the highlights of the rest of the line, and shows us (in reverse order) where it all ends up. Or, to be more exact, with whom.

The Carpenter from Nazareth was the one who came to sort out the situation; to be, as Luke puts it, our

Saviour. His place of temptation was not a lush garden but a dusty desert. Where Adam failed, he succeeded. He had no sin of his own to cover over, so he could deal with ours. Like Abel, he was killed for being God's man. But his blood, as we have seen, speaks not of our guilt but our forgiveness. His death was to atone for our sins. Risen from the dead, he sent his Holy Spirit to indwell his people, to begin to deal with the problem of human nature.

Not long ago I had the privilege of meeting Billy McCurrie. Billy had become a Christian while serving a jail sentence for terrorist offences in Belfast, Northern Ireland. He had found his way into paramilitary activity after his father had been murdered by terrorists on the other side of the conflict, when he was just twelve years old. Revenge was all he could think of. In prison, he had no interest in the things of God. But, strangely, he kept being sent Christian magazines from an anonymous source. In due course, a conversation with the prison medical officer, who was a Christian, made him realize he urgently needed to sort out things with God. He turned to Christ for the forgiveness of his sins; or, as Genesis puts it, he *called on the name of the LORD*. Christ heard his call, and Billy found peace with God. Thrilled with his new life, he wrote to his mother to tell her what had happened. She replied that there was no way she could forgive the people who had shot her husband. Billy wrote back, explaining the facts about Jesus that had changed his mind. A few days later, his mother wrote again. She, too, had turned to Christ, and now felt able to forgive her husband's killers. What politician could bring about a change like that?

Genesis 1–4 only hints at the great Divine solution to our human condition; its main focus is explaining the mess we are in. That solution is the great theme of the rest of the Bible. But these opening chapters have shown us enough to point us towards the answer in Jesus Christ. They have explained our world with unsentimental realism; they have stripped away our human pretensions and excuses; they have introduced to us the majestic, all-sufficient Creator, who is also the Saviour. He calls today to fugitive humanity, as he did in the Garden, 'Where are you?' (3:9). It is time for us to call back.

At that time, people began to call on the name of the LORD. In view of all that Genesis 1–4 has told us, it's the only realistic option if we are to live as we were made to live. Are you doing that today?

Postscript

Taking Genesis seriously

We have now read carefully through Genesis 1–4, and heard its vital message. But along the way, working on the passages, I have been impressed by three remarkable features.

The enormous value of these chapters

First, it is striking *just how much sense Genesis makes of our world*. Again and again through this book, we have moved easily from the Bronze Age to the twenty-first century as we have seen how Genesis applies to us. The gulf between then and now in terms of culture and knowledge is enormous; but Genesis provides a convincing and coherent explanation of so much that we face in our daily experience.

Genesis makes sense of the magnificence of the world we inhabit: it is the work of a brilliant Designer. Genesis makes sense of the widespread suspicion, in many societies, all down history, that there must be a meaning to life; we are not just here as the result of chance.

Genesis makes sense of our world as the product of one, single, organizing mind. We have seen how

Genesis 1 strongly emphasizes the orderliness of the creation, and in so doing laid a vital foundation for modern science. It is very different from some worldviews – held in the religions of ancient Mesopotamia and Egypt as well as in some modern faiths – that understand the world as governed by a number of deities.

Genesis makes sense of the extraordinary dominance of the world by the human race – for good or ill. God has made us in his image, like him, in a position where we exercise rule over our world. We are genetically and therefore anatomically similar to apes, but we dominate in a way they don't. In telling us we have this status, Genesis also makes sense of the only realistic basis for a legal system: one which assumes personal responsibility for one's actions. Genesis is also the foundation for the Christian view of the person, stressing the essential dignity of all human beings and the sanctity of their lives.

Genesis makes sense of the personal embarrassment many find in talking about God: we are not really seeking him but hiding from him. It explains the fact that though many want to call to God in an emergency, we are much more reluctant to yield him our lives.

Genesis makes sense of the extraordinarily mixed nature of life in our world: the perplexing mixture of joy and sorrows, hope and unfulfilled desires that we all experience. Some would say they are just part of the randomness of life in a meaningless world, but if they are not – if there is a meaning, as so much of life suggests – what is it? Genesis explains this as the response of a holy and gracious God to our rebellion, not removing life's blessings but drawing our attention to things being wrong by putting their full enjoyment beyond our present reach.

Genesis makes sense of hatred, and the power of sin to master us; it also makes sense of guilt. It explains why we are the piece of work we are: noble in reason, yet so flawed in character. And so Genesis makes sense of the fact that, despite thousands of years of human progress, and brilliance scientifically, culturally and technologically, we are still at each other's throats.

In all these ways, Genesis makes sense of our world. Of course, in each case there are other possible explanations of some of these phenomena. But Genesis shines for the overall coherence of its account – the way all these different aspects of life are explained *together*. In all the religions of the world, ancient or contemporary, and even in irreligion and atheism, has anyone provided a world view which accounts for so much of human experience in one go, in a way that makes such sense?

This should encourage us to work hard to make the message of these early chapters known. They will help us form a framework in our minds with which to understand our world, and answer people's questions. Above all, these chapters need to be preached – as they were originally given us to be! It would be a disaster if Genesis remained buried beneath a pile of secondary issues.

The focused nature and aim of these chapters

The more one studies Genesis 1–4, the more one realizes that the material is arranged very carefully to make teaching points. The writing is purposeful, selective and focused.

First, the *overall sequence* of these first four chapters has a well-defined flow of thought, with, perhaps, a sharper aim than is sometimes thought. We are introduced, first, to God himself, then to the world, then to our astonishingly privileged place in his plans. Then we are introduced to the right relationship between him and us, and are shown the place of flourishing: in fellowship with him. But next, this relationship with God is broken, and terrible consequences follow: we see the power of sin, and the guilt that follows. Finally, the point is pushed home that, despite human cleverness, only God – the God of the Bible – can sort out the mess. To summarize, *the opening chapters of Genesis are a message preached to the reader about a broken relationship, between God and humanity, setting the scene for how that may be restored, and showing us where to look.* This is Genesis' great, and very practical, purpose.

Given that this is the case, it should not surprise us if some of the things that might interest us – and help us pass science exams – are not on Genesis' agenda. Why should they be? The sad fact is that much of the debate on Genesis has diverted us from seeing what Genesis is really about – and the questions it asks of us.

Secondly, the writer's purpose is reflected in *the way the details are recounted.* The curious note of darkness and desolation in 1:2, answered by God's creation of light, is recounted to stress that he is the God who specializes in creating order out of chaos. In 1:24-25, we saw how the land animals are classified in an unusual way – as *livestock, wild beasts* and *creeping things* – in other words, entirely in terms of how they relate to us – in order to emphasize the importance of humanity in God's plans. It is not that the Bible writers took no interest in the classification of animals – Solomon was famous for knowing about '...beasts, and birds, and reptiles, and of fish.'[1] Rather, it looks as if Genesis has deliberately put it this way to support its main theme: the privileged place God has given us. The instructions about seed-bearing plants in 1:29-30 are there to illustrate what it means for us to be made in God's image.

Genesis is also clearly *selective*: we might long to hear more about the stars, but all we have is the note *and the stars* (Gen. 1:16). 'How? When? Which stars? What about the planets – or the galaxies?', we might ask. Were we in a textbook of science, this would be an extraordinary omission. But Genesis throws this out as a single line, and says no more, as if to stress that what it's really interested in is God and us. Like the best preachers, the writer refuses to be sidetracked.

The *style of writing* also serves the purpose. The account of the days in chapter 1 is structured, almost poetically, to repeat certain phrases which drive home particular themes (God's power, the ordered nature of creation, and so on), and to lead us up to the seventh day. In 2:4–3:24, we saw how the whole account is a great mirror image, with the 'curses' exactly reflecting the blessings of chapter 2, most likely as a way of indicating how all of life has been spoilt.

All these features – both at the large scale and in the details, and in the deliberately selective nature of the account and its style – are there because Genesis is urgent about making, and emphasising, its central message.[2]

---

1.   1 Kings 4:33

2.   For more on how Genesis is pointing in a particular direction, namely to the Lord Jesus Christ, see J. V. Fesko, *Last Things First* (Tain: Christian Focus, 2007).

Grasping this goes a long way to answering the charge that Genesis is 'primitive', or in collision with science. That is not to say that it does not tell us real facts; but it is to tell us that it never intends to be a total account of everything. It is a very purposeful, carefully written account of some things we urgently need to know. At home I have a book called *Be Your Own Lawn Expert*. It is full of vital facts about lawns. But it does not set out to tell me about the whole of the garden. Plants other than grass only enter into things insofar as they encroach on it. There is little about the ecosystem of the lawn, other than the creepy-crawlies that damage the grass. The whole book is shaped around a particular agenda – achieving the perfect lawn. And that's where it stops. In a similar way (though the analogy is inexact), Genesis 1–4 is also selective and agenda-driven. It would, therefore, be unfair to accuse it of being 'primitive' because it does not address all our questions. Equally, we would surely be unwise to press Genesis 1–4 for details it does not supply, which are outside the preacher's purpose.

At this point, a plea. Since Genesis 1–4 is, in all these ways, so clearly focused on teaching us about God, ourselves and our relationships with him and each other, and to point us towards God's solution, surely these great themes must also be the centre of our attention when we teach these chapters? When we argue endlessly about the meaning of the days of chapter 1, for instance, are we in danger of missing the wood for the trees or – dare I say it – of straining out gnats and swallowing camels? Can we keep the main thing the main thing?

The way these chapters point us to the gospel of Christ
There is so much in the opening chapters of Genesis that points us beyond itself – forward to the gospel of Christ. We see, first, that our predicament is both very serious (alienation from God) and one from which we cannot extract ourselves (the way back to his presence is guarded by one with a flaming sword). We are under God's judgment and urgently need his forgiveness. But our natures are so twisted by sin, and our guilt so ineradicable, that we cannot provide the solution ourselves. Yet God's answer is anticipated right here in these first four chapters.

We have seen how, as early as Genesis 1:2-3, God is the God who sorts out the mess. Then, at the end of the opening section, 1:31–2:3, we find that God is the finisher – so again, we should be expecting him, when faced with the disruption created by rebellion, eventually to bring the world back to a state which is *very good*.

Where, and in whom, is this answer to be found? In Genesis 2, the field is narrowed: the God who in Genesis 1 is the Creator of heaven and earth is identified here much more specifically as *Yahweh*, Israel's God, the God of the Bible. It is to him that people begin to call in 4:26, and it is in him that the answer will be found. In Genesis 3:15, there is God's promise of the 'serpent crusher' who will come and overcome the serpent and his evil work – but at terrible personal cost. He will be a human being – the offspring of the woman.

These lines of expectation converge, like spotlights on a stage, on the historical person of Jesus Christ. His perfect obedience is such a contrast to what happened in Eden! He, like Adam, was tempted – but in his case, not in a lush garden but in a dry and dusty wilderness. He, too, was subjected to the tempter's offers and lies. Yet where Adam failed, Jesus succeeded, not once yielding, despite the very attractive prospects the devil set before him.[3] Here, at last, was one who really could conquer the serpent, one who was never personally defeated.

How did he go on to win this great victory? It was, as Genesis predicts, at terrible personal cost: as God had put it to the serpent, 'and you shall bruise his heel.'[4] It took place in an event that looked at first sight anything but victorious: his death on the cross, that first Good Friday. The Bible's astonishing, repeated analysis of this is that this was no accident or heroic martyrdom; rather, he died as our substitute, to take the punishment we deserve for our sin, that we might be justly and freely forgiven.[5]

The Apostle Paul, writing to the Colossians, uses the language of a victory won to describe how Jesus, by his death, dealt with the debt of our sins:

> This he set aside, nailing it to the cross. He disarmed the rulers and authorities and put them to open shame, by triumphing over them in him.[6]

The serpent's wicked work (seen here as that of spiritual *rulers and authorities*) had led to separation between God and people, and our sins stood against us. But now, as Jesus died, that record of sins was cancelled, and the serpent's work was undone, once and for all.

---

3.   Luke 4:1-13

4.   Genesis 3:15

5.   See, for instance, Isaiah 53:6; Mark 10:45; 2 Corinthians 5:21; 1 Peter 2:24

6.   Colossians 2:14-15

There is a further link between Genesis and Jesus' death. In Jerusalem stood the Temple, a building designed to echo the Garden of Eden.[7] The 'holy of holies' stood for the presence of God, but was separated from the rest of the world by a huge curtain, as if to say 'no entry', rather as the cherubim with the flaming sword had done. But at the moment of Jesus' death, this curtain was torn in two, from top to bottom: a clear sign that the way was now open back to God himself.[8] The flaming sword of the cherubim in Genesis 3 had indicated that any attempt to get right into God's presence would meet with certain death; but Jesus, by dying for us, has provided all we need to enter freely.

On the first day of a new week,[9] Jesus rose from the dead. Alive and reigning today, he is at work calling people to himself, and the change he makes in a person's life is so big that Paul calls it a *new creation*.[10] Again, there are echoes of Genesis: what glorious news these first chapters of the Bible point to!

So when we read Genesis, we will not do so simply as a textbook of Christian ethics. Of course, it has (as we have seen) huge amounts to tell us about depending on God, about work, about the value of human life, about taking responsibility, about marriage, about death – and much more. But its biggest purpose is, in the end, to point us to Jesus Christ, that we might find the salvation which he alone has brought.

Nor should we read it impersonally, as if it were of merely academic interest. This ancient text is given for each of us. As

---

7. See 1 Kings 6 and spot the similarities.

8. Mark 15:38

9. John 20:1

10. 2 Corinthians 5:17; Galatians 6:15; see also Ephesians 2:10

it explains who God is, who we are, what has gone wrong, and the first hints of God's solution, it is the beginning of God's call to each of us – to you and me: *Where are you?*[11]

And finally...

The last book of the Bible, Revelation, brings Scripture to an end with notes which consciously echo these opening chapters of Genesis. In his vision, John sees 'a new heaven and a new earth.'[12] There remains a note of warning for those who will not turn to Christ from their evil ways.[13] But for those who have come to seek the answer God gives in Christ, there is a future which echoes Eden:

> Then the angel showed me the river of the water of life, bright as crystal, flowing from the throne of God and of the Lamb through the middle of the street of the city; also, on either side of the river, the tree of life with its twelve kinds of fruit, yielding its fruit each month. The leaves of the tree were for the healing of the nations. No longer will there be anything accursed, but the throne of God and of the Lamb will be in it, and his servants will worship him. They will see his face, and his name will be on their foreheads.[14]

The picture echoes Eden – but now we have no curse. Imagine the present world with the sin and suffering removed: what a picture! In fact, it is not just a picture of Eden restored but something better – for now, there is 'a multitude no one could count, from every nation,

---

11. Genesis 3:9
12. Revelation 21:1
13. Revelation 20:11-15; 21:8
14. Revelation 22:1-4

tribe, people and language.'[15] This is the future Christ has won for us.

The opening chapters of Genesis give us grounds for this great hope. They tell us that God has created the existing heavens and earth – so it must be within his power to make all things new. I may not be able to visualize it, but I am better able to than I would have been before the events of Genesis 1! They introduce us to the God who always finishes his work. Since he has promised to do this, he will.

Truly Genesis 1–4 are the first chapters of *everything*.

---

15.   Revelation 7:9, NIV

FOCUS • ON • THE • BIBLE

GENESIS

THE BEGINNING OF GOD'S
PLAN OF SALVATION

RICHARD P. BELCHER JR.

ISBN 978-1-84550-963-7

Genesis

The Beginning of God's Plan of Salvation

Richard P. Belcher, Jr.

Genesis provides us with a foundation for correctly understanding the world. Within Genesis, the character and the role of human beings within the world God has created is revealed. In reading Genesis we find on every occasion, in his dealings with mankind, God steps in by his grace and demonstrates that he is in control.

> It is hard to think that more material was ever packed into a brief compass, or with greater clarity, helpfulness and ease of reading than Dr. Belcher has managed in this commentary. The words 'thoroughness', 'fairness' and 'lucidity' spring to mind to describe the whole work. Indeed, I cannot think of an important 'stone left unturned'! The treatment, for example, of the creation narrative ranks among the fullest and fairest I have ever read, but, without exaggeration every page has its quota of good things, problems solved, and truths illuminated. In a word, I enjoyed this book from beginning to end and warmly commend it.
>
> Alec Motyer
> Bible expositor and commentary writer, Poynton, England

Richard Belcher is the Professor of Old Testament, Reformed Theological Seminary, Charlotte, North Carolina.

Christian Focus Publications

Our mission statement –

STAYING FAITHFUL
In dependence upon God we seek to impact the world through literature faithful to His infallible Word, the Bible. Our aim is to ensure that the Lord Jesus Christ is presented as the only hope to obtain forgiveness of sin, live a useful life and look forward to heaven with Him.

Our Books are published in four imprints:

CHRISTIAN
FOCUS

popular works including biographies, commentaries, basic doctrine and Christian living.

CHRISTIAN
HERITAGE

books representing some of the best material from the rich heritage of the church.

MENTOR

books written at a level suitable for Bible College and seminary students, pastors, and other serious readers. The imprint includes commentaries, doctrinal studies, examination of current issues and church history.

CF4•K

children's books for quality Bible teaching and for all age groups: Sunday school curriculum, puzzle and activity books; personal and family devotional titles, biographies and inspirational stories – Because you are never too young to know Jesus!

Christian Focus Publications Ltd,
Geanies House, Fearn, Ross-shire,
IV20 1TW, Scotland, United Kingdom.
www.christianfocus.com